The Beginning of Liberalism

Reexamining the Political Philosophy of John Locke

THE McDONALD
CENTER FOR
AMERICA'S FOUNDING
PRINCIPLES

MERCER
UNIVERSITY

THE A. V. ELLIOTT CONFERENCE SERIES

The Thomas C. and Ramona E. McDonald Center
for America's Founding Principles

Guided by James Madison's maxim that "a well-instructed people alone can be permanently a free people," the McDonald Center exists to promote the study of the great texts and ideas that have shaped our regime and fostered liberal learning.

Directors
Will R. Jordan and Charlotte C. S. Thomas
PUBLISHED VOLUMES

No Greater Monster nor Miracle than Myself: The Political Philosophy of Michel de Montaigne, ed. Charlotte C. S. Thomas (2014)

Of Sympathy and Selfishness: The Moral and Political Philosophy of Adam Smith, ed. Charlotte C. S. Thomas (2015)

The Most Sacred Freedom: Religious Liberty in the History of Philosophy and America's Founding, ed. Will Jordan and Charlotte C. S. Thomas (2016)

Promise and Peril: Republics and Republicanism in the History of Political Philosophy, ed. Will R. Jordan (2017)

When in the Course of Human Events: 1776 at Home, Abroad, and in American Memory, ed. Will R. Jordan (2018)

Power and the People: Thucydides' History and the American Founding, ed. Charlotte C. S. Thomas (2019)

From Reflection and Choice: The Political Philosophy of the Federalist Papers and the Ratification Debate, ed. Will R. Jordan (2020)

Liberty, Democracy, and the Temptations to Tyranny in the Dialogues of Plato, ed. Charlotte C. S. Thomas (2021)

The Beginning of Liberalism: Rexamining the Political Philosophy of John Locke, ed. Will R. Jordan (2022)

THE BEGINNING OF LIBERALISM

Reexamining the Political Philosophy of John Locke

Edited by
Will R. Jordan

MERCER UNIVERSITY PRESS
Macon, Georgia
2022

MUP/ P640

© 2022 by Mercer University Press
Published by Mercer University Press
1501 Mercer University Drive
Macon, Georgia 31207
All rights reserved

25 24 23 22 21   5 4 3 2 1

Books published by Mercer University Press are printed on acid-free
paper that meets the requirements of the American National Standard
for Information Sciences—Permanence of Paper for Printed Library
Materials.

Printed and bound in the United States.

This book is set in Adobe Caslon Pro.

Cover/jacket design by Burt&Burt.

ISBN   978-0-88146-837-3

Cataloging-in-Publication Data is available from the Library of Con-
gress

CONTENTS

CONTRIBUTORS

NASSER BEHNEGAR: Associate Professor of Political Science, Boston College, Chestnut Hill, Massachusetts

STEVEN FORDE: Professor of Political Science, Emeritus, University of North Texas, Denton, Texas

WILL R. JORDAN: Associate Professor of Political Science, Co-Director of the McDonald Center for America's Founding Principles, Mercer University, Macon, Georgia

PETER B. JOSEPHSON: Professor of Politics, Saint Anselm College, Manchester, New Hampshire

RITA KOGANZON: Associate Director of the Program on Constitutionalism and Democracy and Lecturer in the Department of Politics, University of Virginia, Charlottesville, Virginia

J. JUDD OWEN: Associate Professor of Political Science, Emory University, Atlanta, Georgia

GABRIELLE STANTON RAY: Instructor of Philosophy, Tulane University, New Orleans, Louisiana

SCOTT YENOR: Professor of Political Science, Boise State University, Boise, Idaho

MERCER UNIVERSITY PRESS

Endowed by

TOM WATSON BROWN
and
THE WATSON-BROWN FOUNDATION, INC.

ACKNOWLEDGMENTS

The essays in this volume were originally presented at the 2020 A. V. Elliott Conference on Great Books and Ideas at Mercer University. This 2020 edition of the Conference proved to be more challenging than usual, however, as the COVID-19 pandemic shut down the world mere days before our scheduled meeting in Macon. At the time, it was by no means certain that the Conference, or this volume, would come to fruition. I am very grateful that the contributors to this volume showed great flexibility and resiliency in seeing the project to the end. The Conference was delayed eight months, took place virtually rather than in person, and then we faced a compressed schedule to get this volume to press. None of it would have been possible without the generosity of spirit and hard work of Nasser Behnegar, Steven Forde, Peter Josephson, Rita Koganzon, Judd Owen, Gabrielle Stanton Ray, and Scott Yenor. I also thank Holly Brewer and Daniel Cullen for their excellent contributions to the Conference.

The Elliott Conference and this book series, now grown to nine volumes, are deeply indebted to the A. V. Elliott family for the generous gift that supports this work. Likewise, we thank Thomas and Ramona McDonald for their generosity in making possible all of the other programming that has established Mercer's McDonald Center for America's Founding Principles as one of the premier academic centers in the Southeast. At Mercer, we are also fortunate to enjoy strong support from our administration, and thank President William Underwood and Dean Anita Gustafson for their efforts on our behalf. I also thank the amazing Charlie Thomas, my co-director at the McDonald Center, for her continued leadership and friendship in this project.

One of the most beneficial and gratifying programs we run through the McDonald Center is our faculty/student reading groups, designed to explore the intellectual themes that eventually culminate in the edited volume. During the 2019–2020 academic year, we read John Locke's *Second Treatise of Government*, *Letter Concerning*

Toleration, and *Some Thoughts Concerning Education* in preparation for the Elliott Conference. I therefore thank Charlotte Thomas, Kevin Honeycutt, Garland Crawford, Meg Donahue, Sarah Gardner, Thomas Scott, Holly Cooper, Tessa Gebert, Michael Hurst, Isabella LeBlanc, Christian Miles, Zachary Mullinax, Matthew Purlee, James Smith, and Ashley Stephens for their wonderful conversation and insights about these books.

I also thank Marc Jolley and his helpful staff at Mercer University Press. The scheduling challenges of this year made this project somewhat more difficult, but Marc and his team still brought everything together like clockwork. The consistent excellence of this series owes a great deal to Mercer University Press.

Finally, I would like to thank my wife Anissa and my sons Evan and Alex. One great consolation to this crazy, COVID year was spending it together.

INTRODUCTION

Will R. Jordan

The language of individual liberty, equal rights, religious freedom, government by consent, and established limits on political power has been prominent in American life since at least the time of the American Revolution and Founding. While these core liberal ideas have never enjoyed anything like a monopoly in American public life, and while American practice has frequently and even shamefully failed to live up to the highest ideals of its liberal creed, there is a strong case to be made that the United States has been uniquely dedicated to liberal political philosophy.[1] We can see it at work in the Declaration of Independence, in Abraham Lincoln's soaring rhetoric, and in the twentieth-century effort to distinguish the American project from its totalitarian rivals. To the extent that America has been guided by liberal political philosophy, it owes something to the thought of John Locke—one of the seventeenth-century founders of what eventually came to be known as liberalism.[2]

Of course, there have been many variations and strains of American liberalism, but it is a testament to the enduring attraction of the Lockean framework that even proposals to fundamentally alter the social contract (another Lockean idea) have tended to

---

[1] Even a partial survey of this debate would require a note longer than this introduction. For a sense of what I mean here, and a clear survey of the ground, see Michael Zuckert, *The Natural Rights Republic: Studies in the Foundation of the American Political Tradition* (University of Notre Dame Press, 1997).

[2] For the American Founders' debt to Locke, see Thomas Pangle, *The Spirit of Modern Republicanism: The Moral Vision of the American Founders and the Philosophy of Locke* (University of Chicago Press, 1990).

adopt the language and emancipatory ends of liberalism.[3] Given this history, we today find ourselves in unusual times, when the major political parties have powerful and growing wings that embrace decidedly illiberal public philosophies. On the Left, critical theory eschews Enlightenment rationalism and liberal ideas of toleration and individual liberty as structures that serve to support inequality and oppression.[4] On the Right, conservative scholars excoriate liberalism for privileging an ideal of individual autonomy that eats away at the civilizing bonds of family, tradition, religion and country.[5] What seems new here is not the critiques themselves, but the power and popularity of political movements that openly and proudly reject the first principles of America's long-dominant public philosophy. Can the center hold? Can the principles of 1776 survive? Or has liberalism run its course?

With these questions in the air, this book proposes to return with fresh eyes to the beginning of liberalism and the political philosophy of John Locke. Instead of looking at Lockean liberalism as a simple and timeworn ideological program, we seek to reexamine Locke's project by remaining alive to the complexity and nuance with which he addressed his subject. The Locke that emerges is indeed an ambitious and radical thinker, but one not as imprudent or

---

[3] See, for example, Franklin D. Roosevelt's 1944 State of the Union Address, proposing an Economic Bill of Rights.

[4] See Robert Paul Wolff, Barrington Moore, Jr., and Herbert Marcuse, *A Critique of Pure Tolerance* (Beacon Press, 1969); Richard Delgado, *Critical Race Theory: An Introduction*, 3rd Edition (NYU Press, 2017); Ibram X. Kendi, *How to Be an Antiracist* (One World, 2019); for examples of how Locke in particular might be approached as a defender of classism and oppression see C.B. Macpherson's classic, *The Political Theory of Possessive Individualism: Hobbes to Locke* (Oxford: Clarendon Press, 1962); and Barbara Arneil, *John Locke and America: The Defense of English Colonialism* (Oxford: Clarendon Press, 1996).

[5] See Patrick J. Deneen, *Why Liberalism Failed* (Yale University Press, 2018); Mark T. Mitchell, *The Limits of Liberalism: Tradition, Individualism, and the Crisis of Freedom* (University of Notre Dame Press, 2018); Yoram Hazony, *The Virtue of Nationalism* (Basic Books, 2018); R.R. Reno, *Return of the Strong Gods* (Regnery Gateway, 2019).

unmindful of custom as his conservative critics would have it, nor as tolerant of oppression as his progressive critics aver.

The book opens with Peter B. Josephson's "The Character of Political Life in Locke's *Second Treatise of Government*." Against those who argue that Locke ignores the messy realities of politics in favor of a sterile approach that is exceedingly formulaic, juridical and legalist, Josephson emphasizes the extent to which Locke does recognize the demands imposed by competing conceptions of justice. Not only does Locke's account of the state of nature reveal an awareness of the difficulties inherent in organizing collective action, but a careful reading of Lockean constitutionalism shows the necessity of managing ongoing conflict between the legislative and executive powers, between both of these and the people, and between the public good and individual interests. Moreover, Josephson sees Locke as acutely aware of the necessity, as well as the difficulties, of cultivating public opinion in ways that strengthen, rather than endanger, the regime's commitment to liberty. Far from ignoring or downgrading political life as being merely ancillary to private goods, Josephson finds in Locke a more robust conception of the character of liberal politics.

In the second chapter, "John Locke's Religious Toleration: The Annapolis Manuscript," Steven Forde examines how a recently discovered manuscript written by Locke in 1667 informs the way we should view Locke's evolving teaching on religious liberty in general, and on the toleration of Catholics in particular. Forde identifies and examines three distinct periods in the evolution of Locke's thought here—the new manuscript shedding light on the middle period—and finds that Locke's increasing willingness to consider tolerating Catholics had little to do with any particular theological or speculative differences, but with a prudential calculation of the threats to a peaceful civic order. As in Josephson's piece, we find a Locke here who is less interested in applying rationalistic political abstractions than in a careful and prudential weighing of competing goods. Ultimately, Forde argues that Lockean principles of toleration have prevailed for so long that we no longer remember Locke's consideration of the practical limits to them. Forde hopes that "Locke's

3

account of the reasons for toleration, and the reasons for those limits, might help guide the cause of toleration today." Included with this chapter is a transcript of the recently unearthed Annapolis manuscript.

Next, we move to what was perhaps Locke's most radical idea, the defense of a right of resistance and revolution. In "Locke's 'Appeal to Heaven:' Jephthah, Conscience, and the Right of Resistance," Gabrielle Stanton Ray examines Locke's frequent use of the phrase "Appeal to Heaven" to characterize the final remedy for those attempting to overthrow tyrannical power. Ray provides here a close reading of Locke's resistance theory, including some interesting caveats and tensions that exist within Locke's account. Foremost among these tensions is Locke's use of the biblical character Jephthah as an illustration of what it might mean to "Appeal to Heaven." Far from being an unambiguous example, Jephthah proves to be highly problematic, guilty of gross violations of natural law and natural rights. Ray concludes from this that the Jephthah example might indicate that Locke "signals a more cautious or conservative attitude toward resistance than is usually attributed him." In other words, a careful reading of Locke again reveals a more circumspect and prudential approach to politics than his seemingly formulaic principles at first suggest.

While recent conservative critics of Locke accuse him of ignoring the importance of tradition or custom in favor of the atomizing fiction of the state of nature,[6] J. Judd Owen's "Locke's Revolution in the 'Law of Fashion'" reveals that Locke is very aware of the power that human beings exert over their fellows through adherence to opinion or custom. In fact, Owen shows that the "Law of Fashion," Locke's term for that which is enforced through a consideration of prevailing opinion, is for Locke much more powerful and effective for human beings than either natural law or civil law. This poses a "fundamental problem for the prospect of directing political society to its proper end as determined by reason and the law of nature." Owen goes on to show that Locke, in his writings on education,

---

[6] See Deneen, 2018, esp. Chapter 1; Mitchell, 2018.

4

argues that any reformation of the Law of Fashion can only take place through slow habituation—rather than rational argument—to a new fashion. Owen thereby poses a series of provocative questions about the true status of reason in Locke's thought, and about Locke's own attempts to cultivate a new fashion.

The subject of education is pursued further in Rita Koganzon's "Why Not Universal Homeschooling? John Locke and the Liberal Objection to Institutional Schooling." Calling into question the charge that Lockean freedom necessitates indifference to the character of the people, Koganzon looks at Locke's criticism of institutional schooling on the grounds that it subjects pupils too much to the opinions and prejudices of their peers (i.e. Owen's "Law of Fashion"). Koganzon elucidates Locke's program of education at home designed to cultivate genuine independence of mind, and also shows how Lockeans of later generations pursued this same goal in ways that were more compatible with the necessities of a mass democratic society. This chapter thereby invites the reader to reconsider what sorts of institutions are most appropriate for the education of a free people.

In his chapter, "Is Locke a Contractual Thinker on Marriage?," Scott Yenor addresses the conservative charge that contemporary family breakdown can be attributed to the Lockean liberal reframing of family relationships in terms of contract. Yenor thinks it "strange to blame a man whose writings appeared in the late 1600s for *today's* problems or to hold the inventor of the modern family—one of the most enduring family forms in history—for its demise." Yenor compares the arguments of the most extreme contemporary marriage contractarians to Locke's version of the marriage contract, and finds that Locke's version is more reasonably constrained by submission to certain "stubborn facts" of nature—including the vulnerability of children and differences between men and women—and by the recognition that the public has a vested interest in family formation. While he prefers Locke's version of the marriage contract to most contemporary accounts, Yenor offers the provocative suggestion at the end of his chapter that it might be a new view of nature, rather than Locke's liberalism or his view of family life, which renders modern thought vulnerable to corrosive revision. This leads us to the book's final chapter.

Undertaking a deep dive to first principles, Nasser Behnegar argues that Locke's ambivalent attitude toward nature may help explain some of the modern world's ambivalence and confusion. Behnegar begins by explicating the view of nature as it was articulated in the Classical and Christian traditions. He then explains how Locke is informed by elements of both traditions, but ultimately "departs in important ways from both traditions." Locke doesn't abandon nature as a standard in some respects, but he displays a radical openness to altering nature in the service of human happiness. For example, "the state of nature is not a model for civil society; it guides its construction the way a problem calls for a solution." Behnegar closes by emphasizing how Locke's ambiguous vision ultimately plays out in his call for a society that encourages the industrious conquest of nature to serve our natural desires for self-preservation.

In the end, these chapters are not designed to offer a definitive treatment of liberalism or of Locke's political philosophy as much as they are meant to serve as an encouragement—to scholars and citizens alike—to revisit the strengths and weaknesses, ends and means, obstacles and opportunities present in Locke's thought. For better and worse, Locke's writings in the late seventeenth century helped inform the philosophy of the American Founding and thereby echo down to us today. If we are indeed engaged in a great debate to determine if liberalism has failed or is worth preserving, we do well to be clear-eyed about how it looked at the beginning. Let us appraise the thing itself, rather than the critics' caricature of the thing. The blessings of liberty might depend on it.

1.

THE CHARACTER OF POLITICAL LIFE IN LOCKE'S *SECOND TREATISE OF GOVERNMENT*

Peter B. Josephson

Introduction

John Locke's *Second Treatise—An Essay Concerning the True Origi-nal, Extent, and End of Civil Government*—was among the principal theoretical sources of political thought at the American founding, and is among the most-read canonical texts of classical liberalism. This makes sense if readers are looking for a theoretical account of natural equality, natural rights, and the foundations of liberal gov-ernment. Yet Locke's text seems to offer very little as a description of the actual activity, motivations, or ethics of liberal political prac-tice. One does not turn to Locke for a characterization of political life of the sort we find in Aristotle, Machiavelli, Tocqueville, or for that matter *The Federalist*. Emily Nacol observes, "We learn very little about the struggles among individuals that surely characterize political societies after the compact is formed; these interpersonal relationships seem to drop out of Locke's formulation of politics."[1] Scholarly accounts of Locke's politics often emphasize either an or-derly collection of free and equal rights-bearing individuals, or an almost juridical account of politics. These accounts suggest that the fundamental political problem—which I take to be the problem of individual and community, diversity and unity, rights and duties (that is to say, the problem of justice)—may be solved, or that Locke believed he had solved it, or was unconcerned with the practical

---

[1] Nacol, "The Risks of Political Authority: Trust, Knowledge and Political Agency in Locke's *Second Treatise*," *Political Studies*, vol. 59 (2011): 592.

problem of the relation between power and justice.[2]

My hope is to move toward a political—and not merely legal or formal—account of Lockean political life as Locke describes that life in the *Second Treatise*. Locke himself was attentive to the phenomenology of politics, and offered an image of what living under liberal politics would be like. I suggest that the image of political life that Locke offers is more dynamic, more tumultuous, and more contested than either the juridical or the legalist interpretations describe, that Locke's liberalism itself does not elide the problem of justice, and that his account of the character of political life as we experience it is more complete than has been appreciated generally.

There is a significant debate among Locke's readers over how we might even categorize, and therefore read, the *Second Treatise*. Some hold that Locke's work offers, in its essence, a normative theory akin to a formal proof in mathematics, and is hardly about the practice of politics at all. In her nuanced and thoughtful work, Ruth Grant, for example, argues that Locke's *Second Treatise* is meant as a mathematical, certain proof of Locke's mixed modes and relations, and is not about the art of governing or an experiential understanding or application of Lockean ethics. The *Second Treatise*, she suggests, offers a "demonstrative normative theory." Thus, Grant finds, the law of nature or reason can provide certainty to ethical norms "because knowledge of our rights and duties . . . can be perfectly known." John Scott adds that Locke shows the way to this moral proof in his account of the reform of language. Through such re-

---

[2] Steven Forde suggests that because Locke defines the public interest liberally—"no more than the aggregation of private, material interests"—he can minimize the problem of the conflict between public and private goods. See Forde's *Locke, Science, and Politics* (Cambridge: Cambridge University Press, 2013), 199. Peter Myers holds, to the contrary, that Lockean liberalism conceives of civil society as having "its own forms and actions," that is, of being more than a collection of private interests and even of establishing its own "regime." Thus, for Locke there is still a tension between public and private goods (*Our Only Star and Compass: Locke and the Struggle for Political Rationality* [Lanham, MD: Rowman & Littlefield, 1998], 180).

form, public discourse itself can be conducted in the language of a mathematically demonstrable moral certainty.[3]

Such accounts typically place reason (of a well-developed sort) at the center of Locke's account of the natural person. Richard Ashcraft, for example, interprets Locke's *Two Treatises* as an attempt "to establish the postulate that the individual in the state of nature is 'a rational creature.'" For Ashcraft the "absolutely crucial" foundation of Locke's political thought is his account of our creation as persons with free will and reason. Locke tells us that the "*Freedom* . . . of Man and Liberty of acting according to his own Will, is *grounded on* his having *Reason*, which is able to instruct him in that Law, which he is to govern himself by" (*2T* 63). Thus the rights-bearing citizen-subjects that Locke describes in the *Second Treatise* must be imagined as rational and moral beings.[4]

We see this tendency to normative or rationalist accounts especially in discussions of Locke's concept of freedom and his theory of consent. In these interpretations Locke's concept of freedom is presented as an account of the "self-transcendence" of morally responsible and well-behaved agents.[5] Some interpret Locke to mean that

---

[3] Ruth Grant, *John Locke's Liberalism* (Chicago: University of Chicago Press, 1987), 14, 19–23; John T. Scott, "The Sovereignless State and Locke's Language of Obligation," *American Political Science Review*, vol. 94 no. 3 (September 2000): 557–8. See also Forde, 234–5, 248. Contrast with these Douglas John Casson's account of Locke's theory of probable judgment, *Liberating Judgment: Fanatics, Skeptics, and John Locke's Politics of Probability* (Princeton; Princeton University Press, 2011), 150–152.

[4] Richard Ashcraft, *Locke's Two Treatises of Government* (Boston: Unwin Hyman, 1987), 121 n.2, 104, 167–8. Parenthetical references (hereafter, First Treatise=*1T*, Second Treatise=*2T*, by section) to Locke's *Two Treatises of Government*, Peter Laslett ed., (Trowbridge, Wiltshire: Cambridge University Press, 1960, 1967, 1988).

[5] Gideon Yaffe, *Liberty Worth the Name: Locke on Free Agency* (Princeton: Princeton University Press, 2000), 6; Peter Schouls, *Reasoned Freedom: John Locke and the Enlightenment* (Ithaca: Cornell University Press, 1992), 29–39; Raymond Polin, "John Locke's Conception of Freedom," in *John Locke: Problems and Perspectives: A Collection of New Essays*, John W. Yolton ed. (New York: Cambridge University Press, 1985), 118.

9

human will is independent of pleasure and pain, or that Locke's persons "are wholly free if their action is guided by their reason." John Simmons calls Locke's theory of tacit consent "a patent absurdity," and promises a new Lockean theory that is "a better, clearer, more helpful view than Locke's own." Like Grant, Simmons argues that Locke subsumed his politics beneath his philosophy, and therefore "wrote relatively little" about governance.[6] In such cases we are led to an interpretation of government by consent that is explicitly not Locke's own, and with a philosophic account of human liberty that is largely unconnected to the experience of the political world. Locke, it seems, was hardly a *political* theorist at all.

Locke's own theory complicates this picture. Most obviously, we learn in the *Second Treatise* that the majority of us are not "strict Observers of Equity and Justice," and are much inclined to put our own interests ahead of others, and even that the law of nature or reason condones such partiality (*2T* 123, 13, 6). Similarly, Locke's philosophic account of the experiences that shape our moral ideas, and thus our capacity for reasoned liberty, begins not with the mind but with the body. The mind cannot receive sensations and contemplate ideas "without the help of the Body" (*ECHU* 2.1.15, 25).[7] The human is a "corporeal rational creature," and our specific corporeality shapes our understanding of ourselves and of the world around us (*ECHU* 2.27.6-8, 15; *ECHU* 4.4.4, 4.11.2).[8] Because we have the

---

[6] These are theories of human action that expressly do not reside in the world of action. Schouls, 145; Andrej Rapaczynski, *Nature and Politics: Liberalism in the Philosophies of Hobbes, Locke, and Rousseau* (Ithaca: Cornell University Press, 1987), 128–35, 154–6; A. John Simmons, *On the Edge of Anarchy: Locke, Consent, and the Limits of Society* (Princeton: Princeton University Press, 1992), 3–4, 9, 92, 199–203. See also his *Moral Principles and Political Obligations* (Princeton: Princeton University Press, 1979), 84.

[7] References to the *Essay* (hereafter *ECHU*) are to book, chapter, and section number. *An Essay Concerning Human Understanding*, Peter H. Nidditch ed. (New York: Oxford University Press, 1975, 1979).

[8] Locke thus distinguishes "personal identity" from "human identity" by attaching to the human the idea of corporeality (*ECHU* 3.11.16; 2.27.21, 29). See Michael Zuckert, *Natural Rights and the New Republican-*

corporeality that we do, we receive the world in a particular way. As Grant observes, in Locke's account our construction of moral ideas is governed by "common human ends." Chief among these common ends is the impulse to self-preservation.[9] This human creature "is concerned for itself" (*ECHU* 2.27.19).

What is at stake here is our own understanding of both the theory and the practice of liberalism. When Locke considers the problem of politics, of the government of human beings, the account he provides is not merely juridical or rational. In the *First Treatise* he warns us that "Ideas of Government in the Fancy, though never so perfect, though never so right, cannot give Laws" (*1T* 81). Locke develops an idea of a constitution or regime that provides not only a formal account of rights and duties, but also an account of political life and a framework for political contestation. Locke is aware, for example, that the use of prerogative "sometimes" gives rise to public disorder (of the sort described in his final chapter), but also "often occasioned Contest" (*2T* 166, 230). How to characterize those frequent political contests remains an open question. In Douglas John Casson's account of the "contested notion of

---

ism (Princeton: Princeton University Press, 1994), 283; and especially Peter C. Myers, *Our Only Star and Compass*, 109–110.

Like other philosophers of the early modern period Locke assayed a "division of the sciences"—an organization of studies under broad headings of Ethics and Physics. It is a complex and apparently incomplete task— Locke made several attempts, including in the final chapter of the *Essay*— and the greatest complexity involves the study of the human. While Locke lists "politica" in the category of "Prudentia"—matters of thought and mind—he lists the subject and agent of politics, "homo," under the heading of "Physica"—matters of the body. For Locke the political lives of human beings mark the intersection of mind and body. In the case of human action, the division between ethics, morals, and reason, on the one hand, and sensations, desires, and bodies on the other is not so neat. In each attempt at a division of the sciences, it is the moment when he arrives at the problem of the human and the political that Locke breaks off his work (See examples from Locke's unpublished Manuscripts and Folios at the Boldeian Library [Ms. C28, 155–158; f41; f50–1]).

[9] Grant, *John Locke's Liberalism*, 40–1.

the public good," the contest is principally between the executive and the people. In contrast, Benjamin Kleinerman describes the fundamental political contest as between the executive and the legislative, with the people as judge.[10] A more robust Lockean account of the causes and motivations of normal political contestation—between legislative and executive, executive and people, legislative and people, and even within or among the people in its role as the common judge—is available to us. Locke is alive to problems we might naturally associate with political life—problems of the conflict between private and public goods (and therefore problems of justice); of ambition, faction, and party; and therefore of the normal managed tumult of political life. As Robert Faulkner writes, "Locke's *Second Treatise* is then much more than some naively legal manual on the mechanics of constitutionalism. It is also and principally a lesson in popular government." Peter Myers goes somewhat further: because Locke makes the purposes of government evident,

---

[10] Casson, 244–252; Benjamin A. Kleinerman, "Can the Prince Really Be Tamed? Executive Prerogative, Popular Apathy, and the Constitutional Frame in Locke's *Second Treatise," American Political Science Review*, vol. 101, no. 2 (May 2007): 220. Casson also makes the important observation that Locke treats "the people" or "the public" as a unity (247–8, 958–9). Kirstie M. McClure also shows Locke's concern to describe the experience of political life, but stops short of a characterization of that life. See *Judging Rights: Lockean Politics and the Limits of Consent* (Ithaca: Cornell University Press, 1996), 233–242. Clement Fatovic sees that Locke's political theory is not only a juridical or legal account, but does not pursue an account of the political struggle that must ensue, in his "Constitutionalism and Contingency: Locke's Theory of Prerogative," *History of Political Thought*, vol. 25, no. 2 (Summer 2004): 287. Shannon Hoff provides a good account of how Locke's political norms shape political practice. See "Locke and the Nature of Political Authority," *The Review of Politics*, vol. 77, no. 1 (Winter 2015): 1–22. Grant finds in Locke's thought a recognition that "there will always be rival political parties," yet she argues that Locke presents a moral scientific solution to the political problem, a solution grounded in "reasoned freedom," moral duties, and a "culture of reasonableness." See "John Locke on Custom's Power and Reason's Authority," *Review of Politics* vol. 74, no. 4 (Fall 2012), 627–9.

his attention is on the means to accomplish those purposes in given circumstances. His is a teaching of political prudence.[11]

Out of the State of Nature

The *Second Treatise* begins by summarizing the *First*, and seems intended to address the political problem that the *First* has described. The conclusion of the *First Treatise* is that political authority as it exists on earth is quite unsettled. Instead, it seems that politics is only the rule of "the strongest." To avoid "perpetual Disorder and Mischief, Tumult, Sedition, and Rebellion" a new foundation for political authority must be discovered and established, "and another way of designing and knowing the Persons" that have political authority properly (*2T* 1). Almost in spite of its avowed purpose to account for the original, extent, and purpose of government, the book concludes with a chapter on "the Dissolution of Government." Such dissolution is to some degree even the result of the exercise of proper powers of political authority (for example, the exercise of prerogative). The structure of Locke's work suggests that he does not finally resolve political problems, or abstract from the experience of politics. The problem of political justice, of the relation between the goods of individuals and the public good, is not solved. Rather, Locke provides a description of a manner of political engagement and the management of political contestation.

In the beginning, Locke's description of the state of nature might suggest that we have no natural need to design and know political authority. The natural condition is one of "perfect Freedom," a freedom to act without "depending upon the Will of any other Man." And it is a state of equality "without Subordination or Subjection" (or "superiority or jurisdiction") of one person to another (*2T* 4, 7). Locke adds that the theologian Richard Hooker recognizes this natural equality and even makes it "*the Foundation of that Obligation to mutual Love amongst Men*" (*2T* 5). The state of nature is

---

[11] Robert K. Faulkner, "The First Liberal Democrat: Locke's Popular Government," *Review of Politics* (Winter 2001): 6; Myers, *Our Only Star and Compass*, 213–220.

governed by a "Law of Nature," and "Reason, which is that Law," is available to anyone who will but consult it (*2T* 6). In the natural condition, a condition in which we imagine there is no established and recognized political authority, this law of nature may be enforced by each individual. It all sounds idyllic.

Yet what at first appears a law of reason that is enforced, as a matter of right, by every individual, quickly descends into a condition of self-serving anarchy.[12] The law of reason actually requires more than mere consultation. The majority are not strict observers of the law. Each man acts as judge in his own case, and his judgment is moved by passion and interest (*2T* 12, 123, 13). "[E]very the least difference" leads to war, and war once begun has no evident conclusion (*2T* 21, 192). This is so not only as a matter of practice but as a matter of right—for example, the right to kill someone who is perceived as a threat (to "kill him if I can"; *2T* 18). There is little peace, and the natural condition "quickly" becomes one of mastery and slavery (*2T* 127). The equality and the freedom of nature—the lack of recognized natural authority—actually begins the contest over authority. The law of nature or reason is not up to the task of governing, and the right to execute that law only perpetuates violence and force. The effect of such execution is not order but war. It is "To avoid this State of War" that political authority and power must be constituted (*2T* 21).

This rhetorical pattern recurs throughout the text. It is almost typical of Locke's style in the *Second Treatise* that normative principles are only a preparation for a more realist account of liberalism.[13]

---

[12] Locke refers to "anarchy" five times in the *Second Treatise* (*2T* 94, 198, 203, 219, 225). Typically, he uses the word in the Greek sense, to describe a condition without a ruler or rule. For example, he contrasts "Anarchy and Confusion" with "Government and Order" (*2T* 203). Similarly, when the executive fails to execute the laws, he has effectually "dissolve[d] the Government," and "this is demonstrably to reduce all to anarchy" (*2T* 219).

[13] This is, in broad perspective, the account of Lee Ward and Ross Corbett. See Ward's *John Locke and Modern Life* (New York: Cambridge University Press, 2010), esp. 101–133; Corbett, *The Lockean Common-*

He gives his readers a comforting entry point (there is a law of nature or reason) only to complicate his account later (the majority of men are not strict observers of equity and justice). Locke repeats this pattern in his accounts of the state of nature, property, consent, the legislative power, the subordination of powers, prerogative, and in a subtle account of the relationship between private and public goods. The pattern itself seems to indicate Locke's awareness of the tension between juridical accounts of the legitimacy of power and prudential accounts of the actual exercise of power.[14]

The moments in the development of the state of nature indicate something of the particular problems that political life is meant to address and the character of political life that Locke envisions. The first of these has to do with the defense and exercise of individual rights; the second with the natural development of private property; and the third with the use and meaning of reason. From Locke's accounts of these natural developments his readers are introduced to the problem of war and civil discord; the dangers of economic inequality and the tension between private and public goods; and the particular qualities or presuppositions about the citizenry that is to be governed.[15]

As Locke presents us, human beings have a capacity and a right to act for the good of others, but naturally they act with attention to their own immediate interests first; this, too, is their right. The duty to others is limited; the individual is *"bound to preserve himself"* and others "when his own Preservation comes not in competition," and each has a right to judge the state of competition for himself (*2T* 6). As a matter of practice the law of nature is asserted in defense of one's own private good. Even in the context of his account of the state of nature Locke begins to draw implications about the consti-

---

wealth (Albany: SUNY Press, 2009), 57ff; Kleinerman, 212; Fatovic, 278, 289.

[14] See also Zuckert, 248; Faulkner, 12; Ward, 102–3.

[15] Locke extends his account of the state of nature through the sixth chapter, and returns to it in the ninth ("Of the Ends of Political Society and Government"), the fifteenth ("Of Paternal, Political, and Despotical Power, Considered Together"), and the sixteenth ("Of Conquest").

tution of government (for example, in his argument that an absolute monarch will act as judge in his own case, and that this disqualifies absolute monarchy as a form of government; *2T* 13). The tendency to subvert the apparent purpose of law continues even in civil society. Locke's first comments about "the positive Laws of Commonwealths" are that they enact "contrary and hidden interests" through "phancies and intricate Contrivances" (*2T* 12). The "Name, Pretences, or Forms of Law" may be manifestly "pervert[ed]" to serve the interest of a particular party (*2T* 20). Human beings are naturally constituted to attend to their self-interest first, and this characteristic is expressed in civil society, too.

The development of natural rights of property and with them of an abundance of goods that can provide for a growing population, and the pre-political invention of money and wealth, are significant events on the path to the establishment of civil society and government. One explicit purpose of this government is the protection of such property rights from the depredations of the quarrelsome and contentious. But the development of the natural rights to property, and Locke's definition of property as encompassing life and liberty as well as estate (a definition he maintains throughout the text; *2T* 123, 173), also reveals a fundamental problem of political justice, which is the relation between private goods and the good of the community, or one's own good and the good of others.

Locke's account of the natural right to property begins easily enough. In the beginning God's donation was "Plenty."[16] Reason and revelation both teach a right of preservation, and because every man has property in his own person the products of his labor are properly and fully his (*2T* 25, 27). Such appropriation of property is

---

[16] Locke uses the phrase "in the beginning" or "at the beginning" six times in this chapter. Both are acceptable translations from the Hebrew Bible (which Locke read). The phrase suggests that the whole chapter might be a gloss on the first book of the Bible, and Locke's use of it seems to demarcate stages of development. See Peter B. Josephson, "Hobbes, Locke, and the Problems of Political Economy" in Michael R. Strain and Stan A. Veuger eds., *Economic Freedom and Human Flourishing: Perspectives from Political Philosophy* (Washington, D.C.: AEI Press, 2016), 9–29.

so clearly right that "there could be no doubt of Right, no room for quarrel" (*2T* 39, 51). The principle of Lockean property rights works, according to Locke, as long as "enough, and as good" is left (*2T* 33). And enough and as good will be left much longer than we imagine, because labor adds so much value to life, liberty, and estate that the one who appropriates to himself actually increases the common pool of resources, perhaps even a thousandfold. We soon learn that the natural condition is actually one of "penury" until human beings labor to improve it (*2T* 32). And property rights in land don't work quite the way that property rights in fruit do. Land becomes scarce, and enough and as good won't be available to others (*2T* 45, 32).[17] And in practice there is plenty of room for quarrel; the right of property is "constantly exposed to the Invasion of others" (*2T* 123). The success of labor and property itself plants the seeds, so to speak, of the trouble to come. The "honest industry of Mankind" becomes subject to "the oppression of power and the narrowness of Party."[18] It is "the great art of government" to address this problem (*2T* 42).

Locke's description of the development of property encounters the tragedy of the commons, and in at least three places Locke suggests that in addition to protecting the rights of private property (of

---

[17] Zuckert, *Natural Rights and the New Republicanism*, 260–2; Alan Ryan, "Locke and the Dictatorship of the Bourgeoisie," in *Life, Liberty, and Property: Essays on Locke's Political Ideas*, ed. Gordon Schochet (Belmont, CA: Wadsworth, 1971), 86–106; Ramon M. Lemos, "Locke's Theory of Property," *Interpretation: A Journal of Political Philosophy*, vol. 5 no. 2 (Winter 1975): 226–44; Gopal Sreenivasan, *The Limits of Lockean Rights in Property* (New York: Oxford University Press, 1995), esp. 31–63; Kristin Shrader-Frechette, "Locke and the Limits of Land Ownership," *Journal of the History of Ideas*, vol. 54 no. 2 (April 1993): esp. 206–11, 215.

[18] In considering the constitution of the legislative, Locke objects to disproportionate representation, and to the tendencies over time for new wealth to be under-represented (and for old or diminished wealth to insist on preserving its power), and for new populations to be under-represented (and for wealth to dominate the political scene, contrary to the principles of equity and fairness) (*2T* 157–8).

"*settl[ing] the Property* which Labour and Industry began"; *2T* 45) it is the role of government to preserve a public commons for use by those who have no estate of their own (*2T* 35), to "regulate the right of property, and the possession of land" (*2T* 50), and even to restore by consent the equality of the natural condition (*2T* 102) in order to remedy the oppression of power and the narrowness of party that naturally arise. In sum, Locke's expectation is that the natural rights of property will lead to contestation in the political arena.

In the natural family, the rearing of children provides both a preparation for and a contrast with civil life. At the beginning of the *Second Treatise* Locke asserts that the ruler of a commonwealth and the father of a family are quite different things (*2T* 2). Parents have "a sort of rule and jurisdiction" over their children, and have an obligation "to inform the mind" of the child, "to regulate his action," and to "prescribe his will" until he attains a presumptive state of reason, and Locke describes this education as preparation for life under civil law as well (*2T* 58-9). Yet this authority of the parents (and "subjection" of the children) is not itself political.[19] Locke indicates some of the capacities of adults in the political community by contrasting those of children. The subject of political authority has a liberty, grounded in a rational pursuit of private interests, which children are not yet capable of. Children lack the capacity to make their own decisions and to "shift for themselves" (*2T* 60). In contrast, a person grown to adulthood and with a capacity to "Reason" is "at his own free Disposal" (*2T* 55). Part of the character of political life is therefore that each is free, equal, and reasonable.

Locke appears to claim that citizens are distinguished from children by their capacity to reason. Locke explicitly excludes from

---

[19] Political power has a much greater reach to regulate property, to bound liberty, and to enforce punishments of death (*2T* 65, 69). Locke is aware that wealth and power can march together. One reason it is "commonly suppos'd" that fathers have political power, or that political power originates in patriarchal power, is that through the governance of inheritance "a Father could *oblige his Posterity to that Government*, of which he himself was a Subject," but Locke makes clear that this is not paternal power, but economic power (*2T* 73).

this condition of reason not only children but lunatics, idiots, innocents, and madmen. Any of these who "comes not to such a degree of Reason, wherein he might be supposed capable of knowing the Law, and so living within the Rules of it, he is *never capable of being a Free Man*" (*2T* 60, 170). It would seem that very much depends on the degree of reason that Locke has in mind. Is Lockean politics the politics of rational men and women? This is a special concern because, as we have seen, in his reevaluation of the state of nature Locke concludes that the majority of people are not strict observers of equity and justice—principles that are promoted by the law of nature or reason—though presumably most people can and do shift for themselves. It would seem from the list of those people Locke excludes that only extreme cases are deemed "not reasonable." Locke's language here is quite precise. In the space of two sections (*2T* 59–60) Locke tells us five times that not reason itself but a supposition or presumption of reason is the benchmark of liberty.[20] At the state of maturity one is "supposed" capable of knowing the law, and "presumed" to know the law. As Richard Hooker explains, the moment when a person has sufficient reason to be capable of being guided by law "*is a great deal more easy for sense to discern, than for anyone by skill and learning to determine*" (*2T* 61). Reason is a problematic test for citizenship because it is difficult to know what reason is and who has it.

For Locke, the test of that condition of reason is not particularly grand; it is the ability "to shift for themselves" (*2T* 60)—that is, to make one's way, to provide for oneself. In *Some Thoughts Concerning Education*, Locke observes that two things fathers want for their sons' education are "wisdom" and "learning" (*STCE* 134). "*Wisdom*"

---

[20] Myers, 215; Peter Josephson, *The Great Art of Government*, (Lawrence, KS: University Press of Kansas, 2002), 57–61. C. B. Macpherson ties rationality to Locke's account of property, and insists that Locke means that only property owners are rational. See his *The Political Theory of Possessive Rationalism: Hobbes and Locke* (Oxford: Oxford University Press, 2011, 1962), 226–238. In contrast Ashcraft finds "no assertion of differential rationality in the text" (175). Macpherson's reading is not sufficiently supported by the text.

in its "popular acceptation" is the word "for a man's managing his business ably and with foresight in this world" (*STCE* 140). This wisdom is different from "*learning*," which Locke notes is "not the chief business" of this education (*STCE* 134, 147, 94). [21] In "Some Thoughts Concerning Reading and Study for a Gentleman" Locke tells us that universal knowledge "is not necessary to a gentleman," and whatever study of morality is offered should be suitable to

---

[21] *Some Thoughts Concerning Education and Of the Conduct of the Understanding*, Ruth W. Grant and Nathan Tarcov eds. (Indianapolis: Hackett, 1996). Hereafter cited as *STCE*, by section. In the same vein, Locke would inculcate a "habit" of justice (understood as respect for property rights) rather than a "reason" of it, because reason is so "rarely obeyed" (*STCE* 110). Just as "*Wisdom*" in that work is treated "in the popular acceptation," so "Justice" as property rights may not be justice itself (*STCE* 110, 140). In the *Essay Concerning Human Understanding*, Locke tells us that "it is not easy to determine of several actions, whether they are to be called *justice* or *cruelty*, *liberality* or *prodigality*" (*ECHU* 2.32.10).

A further example may help describe the distance between popular wisdom and learning. In "Reading and Study" Locke considers whether travel books should be part of the education of a young gentleman, and wonders whether an Englishman will even think foreign travel "worth his time." He adds a passing reference to a "vast number of other travels, a sort of books that have a very good mixture of delight and usefulness." He does not name any of these works (though the reference to delightful and useful works may remind us of his Epistle to the *Essay*) because to do so would require "too much time and room," and these "other travels" are beyond the needs of a gentleman (353). In the *Education* Locke introduces the topic of travel only after telling us that the gentleman's education is complete (*STCE* 212, 214–5). And in the *Conduct of the Understanding* he uses travel and geography explicitly as metaphors for the study of books in science, religion, and philosophy—all of which apparently lie beyond the horizon of the gentleman's education (*CU* 3, 22). Locke's playful pedagogy in the private virtue of curiosity follows a similar course (*STCE* 108, 118, 121, 148). See also Nathan Tarcov, *Locke's Education for Liberty* (Chicago: University of Chicago Press, 1984), 206–7, 171–80; Steven Forde, "What Does Locke Expect Us to Know?" *Review of Politics*, vol. 68 no. 2 (Spring 2006): 254.

"business as a gentleman" and not "as a man."[22] This is a "reason" dedicated to providing for one's own interest in the world.

In each of these cases—in his accounts of the natural law of self-preservation, of the appropriation of the private right of property, and of the direction of reason toward one's own ends—Locke grapples with the tension between private rights and goods and the rights and goods of others (with what he will begin to call the "public good"; *2T* 3, 11, 89, 110, 131). Locke's account of the state of nature thus provides a structure for our consideration of the political problem (the problem of private and public, individual and community) and of the regime and constitution that might address this problem.

Lockean Constitutionalism in Theory and Practice

In each of his accounts of the legislative and executive powers Locke begins almost formally, juridically, but soon develops descriptions of the exercise of those powers that reveal his recognition that political life is not defined by formalism or legalism, but by dynamic political compromises with Lockean principles.

The assertion of the power of the majority to found a government does not at first seem to offer any particular constitutional teaching. Locke tells us that the community may devise any form of regime it wishes (his definition of a "*Common-wealth*" is almost comical), and he offers the usual range of suspects including perfect democracy, oligarchy, and monarchy. But as Faulkner observes, Locke has actually thought beyond the traditional catalogue of regimes. Each regime lays its foundations on the act or will of the majority, and not on any claim from extraordinary virtue, class rule, or one-man rule.[23] Further, as Ross Corbett finds, in the *Second Treatise* Locke begins to use the word "constitution" in a way that is new for him. Rather than verbally—to constitute, as in the *First Treatise*—now the word refers to a form of government, and especially to

---

[22] "On Reading and Study for a Gentleman," in *Political Essays*, Mark Goldie ed. (Cambridge: Cambridge University Press, 1997), 349–51.

[23] Faulkner, 15, 17, 25–6; cf. Myers, 214, 216–17.

the constitution of the legislative power.[24] As Locke unfolds his account of this new constitution its details emerge. Not just any commonwealth will meet the conditions of political life.

Locke's chapter on the legislative power begins in an orderly and juridical fashion, but soon develops into a stage for contestation, ambition, and interests. Initially the legislative is described (at least nine times) as "the Supream Power" and "sacred and unalterable" (*2T* 131, 132, 134, 135, 149, 153, 212). Its enactments are meant to codify for human use the law of nature or reason (*2T* 135). It acts as "Judge on Earth" (*2T* 89, 150, 153). In contrast Locke initially describes the executive power as "derived from and subordinate to" the legislative (*2T* 150).

But the purpose of Locke's chapter "Of the Extent of Legislative Power" is not so much to describe the legislative's unrivalled supremacy in political life as to mark the limits of its power. Locke introduces four such limits: that the legislative power must enact laws in keeping with the law of nature and for the public good (*2T* 135); that it must promulgate or publish those laws, and that they must be standing laws and not temporary or arbitrary decrees (*2T* 136–7); that it cannot institute taxation without consent (*2T* 138–40); and that it cannot transfer the power of making laws (*2T* 141). At the end of the chapter Locke inverts the first two items on this list, placing settled and promulgated laws first, and laws for the public good second. When he first introduces the condition that the legislative power must make law for the public good, Locke references the law of nature as a guide for that legislative work five times. When at the end of the chapter he inverts the first two limits he includes no explicit reference to the law of nature or reason at all (*2T* 135, 142). The law of reason that is to precede and guide the civil law seems absent.[25]

---

[24] Corbett, 57.

[25] Josephson, 219–225; Corbett, 54–5. Cf. Myers, 219; Simmons, 62 n.10; Fatovic reads the law of nature and the public good as equivalents, and therefore finds no difficulty in the alteration Locke makes (284). I read the passage differently in part because the law of nature carries an obliga-

Locke also makes a significant modification to the principle of the consent of the governed. Locke provides two accounts of the movement out of the state of nature. One of these is anthropological or historical. The other involves an act of individual consent to establish a society "wherein a *Majority* have a Right to act and conclude the rest" (*2T* 95). In the first section of the *Second Treatise*, Locke tells us that he seeks a foundation for government other than force and violence (*2T* 1). When he introduces the teaching of majority rule he tells us that the majority has the greater force (*2T* 96). The absence of violence is, at least, an improvement over the foundation in force and violence, but the explanation from force suggests that Locke is aware of and realistic about the ethic of majority rule.[26] The movement from individual consent to the rule of the majority also catches our attention. Locke is, again, careful with his language: "*the act of the Majority* passes for," or is "received" as the act of the whole community (*2T* 96, 98), but it is not precisely the act of the whole or of each individual. In practice and as a matter of prudence the Lockean principle of individual rights and consent must conform to the realities of political power. Locke's text signals an awareness that the consent of the individual, the consent of the majority, and the consent of the public as a whole are three different things.

Similarly, Locke begins his account of the taking of property, or the tax power, with a very strongly worded rule. "*The Supream Power cannot take* from any Man any part of his *Property* without his own consent" (*2T* 138). In the next sentence Locke moves from asserting the necessity of the consent of each individual to emphasizing the consent of the people in the plural—"their own consent." Two sections later Locke clarifies what "his own Consent" means in practice. Taxation must be "with his own Consent, *i.e.* the Consent of the Majority...or their Representatives" (*2T* 140). What seemed

---

tion to all mankind, but the public good involves an obligation to a particular conventional community that is preferred to the rest of mankind.

[26] See also Thomas Pangle, *The Spirit of Modern Republicanism* (Chicago: University of Chicago Press, 1988), 254–5.

at first an extraordinarily strong, and practically unworkable, rule is amended in such a way that taxation becomes practically possible, but only at the apparent sacrifice of the principle of individual consent.[27]

Locke's account of the development of legislative power suggests that it is a mistake to consider the legislative as simply representative of the people. In the course of first listing the limits on the legislative power Locke cautions that legislators might "think themselves to have a distinct interest, from the rest of the Community" (*2T* 138). By the time he concludes his account Locke warns that the legislators will not only think they have a distinct interest from the public, but will in fact "come to have a distinct interest from the rest of the Community," and will make the law "to their own private advantage." Indeed, the representative assembly, having neglected the law of nature (and perhaps the public good as well), may "grasp at Power" (*2T* 143). Elections are therefore not only about the public's choice of representatives, but the public's check on them (*2T* 154, 158).[28] Occasionally Locke implies a contest between the legislative and the people who feel unrepresented. The people, or a part of them, may come to feel that there is one rule for the countryman at plow and another for the favorite at court. Early in his description of the constitution of the legislative and executive powers Locke writes, "[T]hus the *Community* perpetually *retains a Supream Power* of saving themselves from the attempts and designs of any Body, even of their Legislators" (*2T* 149). The people may "remove or alter" a legislative power that acts contrary to its trust. In the end the people have a power to resolve their dispute with a usurping legislative body by erecting a new legislative power (*2T* 220), or a new form of legislative power, or by placing the old form in new hands (*2T* 243). Each of these are acts of resistance.

---

[27] Compare Grant, who calls this part of Locke's argument "formal, legalistic," and "hollow" (81), and Simmons, who concludes that Locke's assertion "is not a very good argument" (92).

[28] Faulkner, 27; Pangle, 255. Rather than representing a unity or harmony of the community, the legislative weighs conflicting interests or goods (Myers, 218–19).

Yet the most obvious political contest within the context of Locke's account of the constitution of the powers of government is between the legislative and the executive. The executive exists to remedy several defects in the legislative power. There are dangers in having a legislative power always in session—a danger that the laws will be changing and not standing and settled, and that the members of the legislative will never return to the status of citizens subject to the law as others are. On the other hand, the law cannot be enforced only sometimes, when the legislative is in session. As a practical matter, then, the power to make law and the power to execute the law must be separated, and in part for these reasons "all moderated monarchies, and well-framed governments" place the executive and legislative powers in separate hands (*2T* 159, 144, 153). But Locke does not describe only a separation of these powers. In one prominent example the executive aims directly at reforming the corruption of the legislative which, on Locke's account, is bound to creep in.[29] Representation "becomes very *unequal* and disproportionate to the reasons it was at first establish'd upon," and this disorder arrives "insensibly, as well as inevitably" with the passage of time (*2T* 157–8). "[P]rivate interest" often preserves customary distributions of power "when the reasons of them are ceased" (*2T* 157). As a result "one part, or Party" subjects the rest. Locke attributes this tendency toward "Corruption, or decay" in part to the constant flux of the world, especially the flux of wealth and population, and in part to the distance that develops over time between the private interests of some legislators and the public good (*2T* 157, 143, 158). In this circumstance the executive has a prerogative to reform "the true proportion" of representation.[30] Such reform is bound to be re-

---

[29] Myers argues that Locke's division of political powers comes from the recognition that no one person, or one branch of government, or we may say one particular interest, can embody all reason. In our experience, reason is partial and interested (224). Ward concludes that "the most significant theoretical achievement of Locke's reflections on government is his conception of a legal power to control the legislative power itself" (105).

[30] There has been extensive debate about what this "true proportion" is. Locke speaks of legislative apportionment based on considerations of

sisted by the dominant legislative power.

Locke goes further, however, to specify that the executive power actually is meant to address certain defects inherent in the rule of law itself. No lawmaking power, and no human power, can foresee all the necessities and accidents that may arise; emergencies, particularly in the area of national defense, cannot wait until the legislative provides for them (*2T* 157, 159). In addition to these limits of foresight, Locke offers two other explanations that describe something of the requirements of executive power, and of the character of political life. Locke argues that "Many things" (or "accidents") cannot be provided for by law at all because the political world is subject to so much flux or motion that the law may prove defective or misdirected over time. The law that is appropriate at one time may not be so when the times change (*2T* 157).[31] Second, what is good or right generally may not be good or right in particular cases. "[A] strict and rigid observance of the Laws may do harm" because the law "makes no distinction of Persons" (*2T* 159).[32] The rule of law is not always a proper vehicle for weighing public and private goods, and a continual public wrangling over how law can meet the flux of political life is inevitable. Together these two critiques of a strict rule of law suggest that the politics Locke has in mind includes uncertainties and disputes over the application of the law and the weighing of public and private goods. Prerogative is necessary to introduce prudence and discretion into government as corrections to the standing

---

"Wealth and Inhabitants" (*2T* 157). Seliger and Macpherson argue that Locke means to base the apportionment of legislative seats on wealth alone, and even disenfranchises the majority of inhabitants (Martin Seliger, *The Liberal Politics of John* Locke (Praeger, 1969) 286; Macpherson, 248–9). Ashcraft and Faulkner point out—with greater fidelity to Locke's text—that even "the meanest Men" have a share in the legislative (*2T* 94, 158; Ashcraft, 171, 177–8; Faulkner, 28).

[31] As Fatovic explains, in part for this reason an account of political life cannot be only "legalistic" and "judicial" (278–9, 282). See also Grant, 2–3; Corbett, 68–9, 127–8; Kleinerman, 214.

[32] As Corbett emphasizes, the law may actually punish a man who deserves reward (76–7).

positive law (*2T* 147). It is, in practice, a wholly political power, one bound only by limits of political prudence and political contestation.

To the first executive power of enforcing the law (*2T* 144) Locke adds five categories of prerogative power.[33] The five powers are the power to conduct defense and foreign policy (*2T* 147); the power to convene legislative sessions (*2T* 153–6);[34] the power to reapportion legislative seats (*2T* 157–8); the power to pardon offenders (*2T* 159); and the power to act without or prior to a law,

---

[33] Corbett, intriguingly, distinguishes executive power from prerogative power because executive power is derived from a legislative authority but prerogative power is founded directly on the common law of nature (*2T* 159; Corbett, 79–80; compare Josephson, 242).

Though Locke does not explicitly describe foreign relations as coming under the prerogative power, this "power of war and peace" certainly fits the criteria he establishes for a prerogative power. Locke tells us that this "Federative" power is "really distinct" from the executive but also that the two are "always almost united," and that "it is much less capable to be directed by antecedent, standing, positive Laws, than the Executive." The federative power is subject to "Prudence" more than to law (*2T* 147). Corbett, to the contrary, argues that the federative power is different from prerogative because it is exercised in regard to people outside of the political community; legal authority to act is not really a question. Corbett also argues that federative power is subject to legislative judgment in a way prerogative power is not (Corbett, 81; *2T* 153). But prerogative, it seems to me, is subject to legislative judgment and contestation, and to the common judgment of the public (*2T* 159, 240). I therefore count the federative power among the exercises of prerogative.

[34] Fatovic (281) and Corbett (72–3) each find that Locke establishes prerogative powers both to convene and dismiss the legislative. On my reading Locke suggests a fixed calendar for legislative sessions and a prerogative to convene special sessions. The executive has the power to convene the legislative "when there is need of it" (*2T* 155; Josephson, 226–8). Indeed, Locke singles out the executive who hinders the legislative from meeting as one who has committed an offense that justifies resistance (*2T* 155, 215). This reading is justified as well by the historical abuse of the power of dismissing the legislative in England during the seventeenth century. Thus, when Locke describes the power to both convene and dismiss the legislative, he uses the past tense (compare *2T* 154 with *2T* 156).

and "sometimes even against" the sanction of law "for the publick good" (*2T* 160, 164, 166, 210).

There are very clear parallels between the five prerogative powers and the five causes of the dissolution of government that Locke describes in his final chapter. Those causes are that an executive may put his own arbitrary will in place of the laws (*2T* 214; that is, may act without or contrary to the law); that the executive may hinder the legislative from meeting (*2T* 215, 155; that is, may dismiss the legislative assembly); that the executive might alter the manner of election (*2T* 216; that is, may abuse the power to reapportion the legislative); that the executive may deliver the people into subjection to a foreign power (*2T* 217; that is, may abuse the federative power); and that the executive may fail to execute the law (*2T* 219; that is, may abuse the prerogative to pardon). The acts that some will view as proper exercises of prerogative others will consider alterations of the legislative and executive powers, usurpations that justify resistance.[35] Even legitimate uses of prerogative, and even mere "attempts" or "Endeavours" to exercise executive prerogative, may be read as abuses of the sort that "often occasioned Contest, and sometimes publick Disorders," perhaps especially when "private" and "factious" men, or "Flatterers," promote that reading to the public (*2T* 94, 166, 195, 221, 230, 239, 240). There is even a possibility of "endless contention and Disorder" (*2T* 106). To the objection that he is authorizing frequent political contestation, Locke's answer is, in effect, yes; such is the nature of political life. "*The People* . . . will wish and seek for the opportunity" of resistance, "which, in the change, weakness, and accidents of humane affairs, seldom delays long to offer itself" (*2T* 224). In Locke's account, political contestation, short of resistance or revolution, is actually quite common.

The Common Judge

One great reason for the establishment of civil society is the institu-

---

[35] Josephson 2002, 236–8; Casson 2011, 245, 251. Leonard Feldman has a similar finding in "Judging Necessity: Democracy and Extralegalism," *Political Theory* (August 2008): 559–560.

tion of a common judge with authority to decide controversies (*2T* 21). Because "it is unreasonable for Men to be Judges in their own Cases" (due to "Self-love," "Ill Nature, Passion and Revenge"), in a properly political society "all private judgment of every particular Member being excluded, the Community comes to be Umpire" (*2T* 13, 87). It is the "common judge" that delineates the difference between the state of nature (or war) and civil society (*2T* 91). A common judge would seem to solve the problem of sovereign authority, and yet the liberal community is marked especially by contentious claims of right by individuals and minorities. These claims are subject to public judgment, but the way in which the public exercises its judgment proves deeply problematic.

On one occasion Locke speaks of the legislative power, or the legislative and executive together, as playing the role of common judge (*2T* 88–89, 150), but neither the legislative nor the executive can fulfill this role. The legislative could abuse its powers (could "go about to enslave or destroy" the people), and then there does not seem to be a common judge between the legislative and the people (*2T* 168). This is true of executive prerogative as well. Generally the first commonwealths were under the government of one man, a result of the experience of paternal affection and the custom of obedience. In this earlier golden age, governors "had more virtue" and subjects were "less vicious" than they are in modern political life. (This in itself is a lesson about the character of our politics.) "Experience" taught lessons about "Ambition and the Insolence of Empire," "Covetousness" and "evil Concupiscence," and the "Encroachments of Prerogative, or the inconveniences of Absolute Power" which are the natural tendency of monarchy (*2T* 94, 105–107, 110, 111). "[W]eak princes" use prerogative "for private ends of their own, and not for the publick good" (*2T* 162). And in disputes over the exercise of prerogative Locke observes that there can be no judge between the executive and the legislative (*2T* 165, 168).[36]

---

[36] On the one hand the institution of a common judge seems "crucial to Locke's account of the establishment of political society" (Ashcraft, 112). On the other hand a common judge would seem to have the function

Locke's chapter on prerogative concludes with the question of who shall judge the proper use of this power, and Locke's answer is that there is no sovereign judge on earth. In such circumstances the people are left with an "*appeal to Heaven*," a well-known Lockean euphemism that typically ends in war. But here Locke makes a surprising turn. Not only does "the Body of the People" have the liberty to make such an appeal; "any single Man" does as well (*2T* 168).[37] The individual does not abandon the natural right of preservation upon becoming a member of society (*2T* 129, 131). As Locke unfolds his reasoning we learn that the people's right to appeal to heaven, to judge the exercise of prerogative, is predicated on the right of the individual. Locke repeats this induction twice. It is because an individual has an inalienable right to preservation that we may conclude that the people does as well (*2T* 168). He applies a similar induction at the end of the final chapter, where the judgment of whether to appeal to heaven rests with "every Man" and thus with "the People" (*2T* 241, 242). The chapter on prerogative thus concludes with the reassertion of a natural right of self-preservation, a right held both by each individual and (now) by "the People" as a body. Later Locke will describe this as society's "Native and Original Right...to preserve itself" (*2T* 220). It is a native right to judge the exercise of prerogative—a power Locke also describes as "natural."

Locke speaks fairly easily of the public interest or the public good (and on one occasion of the "common good"; *2T* 131), but he also speaks of "the public" as a political actor in its own right. He does so as early as the Preface to the *Two Treatises*, where he decries those who have espoused the work of Sir Robert Filmer as having

---

of a sovereign, and yet Locke has told us that neither the legislative nor the executive, nor even the rule of law itself, is sovereign. There is no final judge on earth (Grant, 75-8). See also Scott, who draws our attention to Locke's comment that this is an "inconvenience" (another Lockean euphemism—for "Evil" [*2T* 13]) that troubles all governments (*2T* 209; Scott, 553).

[37] Ashcraft, 182–3; Scott, 551–2; Josephson, 138–9. Compare Casson, 247; Nacol, 589.

"done the Truth and the Publick wrong." Later Locke asserts that "there and there only is a Political, or Civil Society" where everyone has resigned his natural executive power to "the publick" (*2T* 89). He writes of the legislative "which the publick has chosen and appointed" (*2T* 134). The federative power manages the *"interest of the publick"* in its relations with other states (*2T* 147).[38] The executive-federative power wields the "Force of the Publick" (*2T* 148). One reason that justifies the prerogative of the executive is that no legislation can foresee "all Accidents and Necessities, that may concern the publick" (*2T* 160). The danger of executive prerogative is that it may "make or promote an Interest distinct from that of the publick" (*2T* 164). Prerogative is accepted when the executive acts visibly in "care of the publick" (*2T* 165). In these instances, "public" really works as a noun.

In some cases Locke nearly conflates the good of the public or community with the good of individuals. For example, prerogative is for the good of the community, and the community is established for the "mutual good" of its members (*2T* 163). In that pivotal chapter "Of the Ends of Political Society and Government," which begins the second half of the book, Locke seems to suggest first that there is a harmony of public and private goods in the political society that he describes. In political society natural power is relinquished to the political community "so far forth as the preservation of himself [the individual], and the rest of that Society [the collective] shall require" (*2T* 129). A member "wholly *gives up*" the natural power or right to execute the law of nature in order to provide for himself and for "the good, prosperity, and safety of the Society" (*2T* 130). And in the next section Locke again conflates *"the common good"* (the only time that phrase is used in the *Second Treatise*) and "the good of the

---

[38] In introducing the federative power Locke first argues that before a federative power is conceived one must imagine a community that is distinct from the rest of mankind. "[T]hey make one Body, which is, as every Member of it before was, still in the State of Nature with the rest of Mankind. Hence it is, that the Controversies that happen between any Man of the Society with those that are out of it, are managed by the publick" (*2T* 145).

society" with the preservation of one's own (private) liberty and property (*2T* 131).

This offering soon gives way to an acknowledgement of the distance and even the tension between these goods, or the problem of justice. His consideration of the prerogative to convoke the legislative assembly is framed in the context of the public good, and not the good of particular individuals (*2T* 157, 167, 222). At other times he recognizes a tension and even conflict between the public good and the good of the individual, as when it is necessary to tear down an innocent man's house to stop the spread of fire through the community; in that context the "*end of Government*" is the preservation of all the members of society but only "as much as may be" (*2T* 159). In a similar vein he tells us that "the *first and fundamental natural Law* . . . is *the preservation of the Society* and (as far as will consist with the publick good) of every person in it"—which suggests that in the end the two are not fully consistent (*2T* 134). Perhaps most importantly, the individual's judgment that his rights have been violated and the public's judgment of his claim may be quite different (*2T* 208–9). In each of these examples Locke seems to recognize cases in which the good of the public and the good of the individual diverge. He is aware of the fundamental problem of politics, and he seems aware that a liberal account of individual rights as a subject of public judgment has not solved that problem.

The endorsement of the public as common judge seems to set aside a significant problem—that in the natural condition the majority are not strict observers of equity, justice, and the law of nature or reason (*2T* 123). In the *Essay*, Locke tells us that this circumstance is "unavoidable"; the majority can shift for itself but it is not capable of reasoning in the strong sense. Rather it must "be persuaded of several opinions whereof the proofs are not actually in their thoughts" (*ECHU* 4.6.2). Moreover, this majority will not be persuaded by "an argument," even or perhaps especially by a well-reasoned argument. They are governed instead by customs, traditions, and beliefs (*ECHU* 4.16.3–4).[39]

---

[39] Josephson, 262–3.

The problem of the majority's judgment will not matter, in theory, if Locke means to treat consent and dissent as the hypothetical judgments of a rational person. By this interpretation Locke does not claim that political authority is rooted in the actual consent of actual citizens and subjects; rather, Locke effectively asks what a reasonable person would consent to. This makes quite a lot of sense. Locke tells us that the "*Freedom* then of Man . . . is *grounded on* his having *Reason*" (*2T* 63). An unreasoned "consent" does not seem really consensual, any more than a coerced consent does.[40] The majority cannot consent to just anything; it, too, is bound by the law of reason. To found the legitimacy of government on the consent of the unreasonable would itself seem unreasonable, and perhaps even illegitimate. The true standard of legitimacy is therefore governance in accord with the law of reason.

But there are good reasons to think Locke has in mind a way to weave together something like the hypothetical consent of the rational person with something like the empirical consent of actual human beings. As we have seen, politically speaking, rationality may not mean much more than an ability to shift for oneself. Moreover, the argument that Locke means a hypothetical rational agent seems to set aside his foundations of natural rights to life, liberty, and estate, and especially to self-preservation. The argument from natural rights is that, as there is no natural authority, so individuals have a natural right to preserve themselves, and a natural right to judge of their preservation for themselves. Indeed, this is the first precept of the law of nature or reason, and it is alienated upon entering civil society only "so far forth as the preservation of himself, and the rest of that Society, shall require" (*2T* 6–7, 129).[41] Nor does it seem the

---

[40] See especially Hanna Pitkin, "Obligation and Consent I," *American Political Science Review* (1965): 995–999; John Dunn, *The Political Thought of John Locke: An Historical Account of the Argument of the Two Treatises of Government* (New York: Cambridge University Press, 1969); John Zvesper, "The Utility of Consent in Locke's Political Philosophy," *Political Studies* (March 1984): 58; Scott, 558.

[41] See especially Patrick Coby, "The Law of Nature in Locke's *Second Treatise*: Is Locke a Hobbesian?, *The Review of Politics*, vol. 49 no. 1 (Win-

case that consent matters only at the founding. Shannon Hoff identifies five instances in which Locke applies the norm of consent to the operations of political life: through the establishment of the legislative power and its limits; in adherence to the natural law of self-preservation; in the exercise of executive power and the public's judgment of such exercise; in the preservation of property rights; and in the rights of conscience and resistance.[42] On Locke's account the question of a common judge—of the representative quality of the legislative power, of the authority granted to exercises of prerogative, and of appeals to heaven—is a recurring question or work. Locke's concern is not only for the moment of founding but also for an ongoing political practice or construction of consent.

In Locke's hands consent is not only a matter of right, but also itself an instrument of governance. As a matter of right, government requires the consent of the governed (*2T* 95). As a matter of prudence, winning consent may be the best fence against popular resistance. Political rule, strictly understood, requires governance by "established laws of liberty." To rule in that way is "the great art of government" (*2T* 42). When one recognizes that arguments and authority—and insolence, imperiousness, and "the magisterial air"—do not persuade, then one must adopt the "gentle and fair" way of persuasion. In politics and in education the work is to lead the public toward what is reasonable, even though men themselves are very often not reasoning. In the *Education*, Locke recommends a milder method of governance and the adoption of an egalitarian carriage as the means of effective persuasion (advice that he also offers in the *Essay* 4.16.4; *STCE* 95). To lead young men to reasonable behavior, the tutor, or "governor," must act with the quality of "discretion" (*STCE* 90). In his discussion of the use of prerogative in the *Second Treatise*, Locke speaks of the need for discretion four times (*2T* 159, 160, 162; see also *2T* 94, 111). Reason thus enters impassioned political life quietly and indirectly—discretely—by shaping customs

---

ter 1987): 4–6. On the inalienable natural right of preservation, see also Zuckert, *Natural Rights*, 246, 365; cf. Simmons, *Anarchy*, 118.

[42] Hoff, 18–22.

and habits of opinion and behavior (or in another example, in the replacement of "Custom" with "Reason" in the reapportionment of legislative seats; *2T* 157).[43] Attention to rights of life, liberty, estate, and preservation wins consent, and consent makes governance itself more secure. Locke's theory of consent is a teaching both of what is right and what is prudent.

But political life is never simply reasonable, or the work of rational agents. Locke introduces a new liberal language into civic discourse—the language of natural rights, equality, and constitutionalism—but this innovation will produce a reasoning public only in the sense of its ability to shift for itself.[44] Language suggests logos. But Locke emphasizes that language has two uses that are "very distinct" (*ECHU* 3.9.3, 15). Civil language facilitates the "ordinary affairs and conveniences of civil Life." Philosophic language aims to "convey the precise Notions of Things" (*ECHU* 3.2.1, 3.9.3, 3.5.6). Locke counsels that in public life we ought not to expect the exactness of philosophic inquiry (*ECHU* 3.11.10). "[M]ost Men" will consider the toil of philosophy "very troublesome" (*ECHU* 3.11.9). "[E]specially in moral matters" therefore the "Reason" of most men is "empty," "obscure" and "not regularly and permanently united in Nature" (*ECHU* 3.10.4). The uncertainty of civil speech—its lack of philosophic precision—subjects interpretation of the laws to obscurity and confusion (*ECHU* 3.9.9, 22). This confusion especially afflicts political life, where it unsettles "Peoples Rights." Moreover, language is a construct requiring consent, and thus no single reformer has the power to impose words or ideas on others (*ECHU* 3.2.8, 3.9.8). Locke asks, "Who shall be the judge" of the right meaning of a word when each "with Reason thinks he has the same

---

[43] To the extent that reason might have a share in governance, it governs through the inculcations of habits and customs. See especially Ruth Grant, "Custom's Power and Reason's Authority," *Review of Politics*, vol. 74 no. 4 (Fall 2012): 607–627; Tarcov, 214; compare Nacol, 591; Forde, "What Does Locke Expect Us to Know?" 248–9, 255–6; Josephson, 261–6, 279–80.

[44] Scott (557–8) and to some extent Kleinerman (219–220) count on the new language to produce a new public reason.

right" to judge? It is almost impossible for language to "obtain a general consent" and at the same time to satisfy "a considerate inquisitive Person" (*ECHU* 3.6.27).[45] Reasoned speech is subject to public judgment, and public judgment responds to pathos more readily than it does to logos. Locke's constitutional language establishes the terms of the political contest: just and equal representation; rights of life, liberty, and estate, and perhaps religion; and the weighing of public with private goods. But these terms only frame the contest; they do not decide it.

Not even the experience of tyranny produces a public that is reliably vigilant and dependably reasonable. Locke reminds us that even with such an experience the "People are not so easily got out of their old Forms, as some are apt to suggest." It is not an easy thing to move the public to address "defects . . . or corruption" in government, "even when all the World sees there is an opportunity for it." The people are slow and averse to political action with the result that "in this and former Ages" and "after some interval of fruitless attempts" England remains with its old constitution (*2T* 223, 230).[46] The natural right of preservation, and its implicit but con-

---

[45] For a full treatment of this topic see Michael Zuckert, *Launching Liberalism: Locke's Political Philosophy* (Lawrence, KS: University Press of Kansas, 2002) 107–126.

Locke offers five remedies for the defects of language, but each of these proves inadequate (*ECHU* 3.11.8–27). The first two aim at clarity in thinking (*ECHU* 3.11.8–9). The third remedy is to use the common or public signification of words to gain an "entrance into other Men's Minds with the greatest of ease," but then the old words will only be heard as old ideas (*ECHU* 3.11.11–12). The fourth is to construct new but carefully defined words, but in public discourse these arouse suspicion (*ECHU* 3.11.12–25). It is virtually impossible to follow the fifth, and be constant in our use of words (*ECHU* 3.11.27). These suggestions—using old words with new meanings, or combining ordinary words in a way that confounds their ordinary meaning (*ECHU* 3.6.51)—are later examples of abuses of language (*ECHU* 3.10.6, 3.10.23).

[46] In the third edition Locke wrote that the people might erect a "new form, or new hands" for the legislative power. In the fourth edition he wrote that the people might "erect a new form, or under the old form place

comitant right of resistance, will not lay "a perpetual foundation for disorder" because—in practice—the right of an individual or minority will not cause public inconvenience until "the majority feel it, and are weary of it, and find it necessary to have it amended" (*2T* 168, 132, 209, 230).[47]

The public's judgment is rooted in a sensation of politics, what McClure describes very finely as the "sensory and experiential character of political judgment."[48] Locke tells us that the public (or the majority) can be led to "see and feel" the effects of tyranny (*2T* 209, 223, 268). In one case when he refers to the public's "sence of rational Creatures" Locke then immediately clarifies that the public "think[s]" as it "feel[s]" (*2T* 230). When sensations become a common sense then the public renders its judgment. Political judgments, in such instances, are affective, and the public derives such judgment from the felt effects of government. Public judgment is not reasoned, but it may be led to an imitation or approximation of what is reasonable.

Locke provides clues about what will move the majority's judgment that tyranny is afoot and that political action is needed. Most evidently, the majority may be roused to action when it feels a threat "that their laws, and with them their estates, liberties, and lives are in danger, and perhaps their religion, too" (*2T* 209, 225).

---

it in new hands," a clarification that acknowledges the disappointing difficulty of correcting the constitution. See *The Two Treatises of Government*, Mark Goldie, ed. (London: Everyman, 1993), 257.

[47] Locke reiterates this reality later, near the end of the chapter on tyranny. "[T]he right of resistance" will not usually cause sudden disturbances of government. "Private men . . . have a right to defend themselves," but it is "impossible for one, or a few oppressed men to disturb the government, where the body of the people do not think themselves concerned with it" (*2T* 208). As Scott explains, "Locke's reason for usually speaking of popular instead of individual resistance has more to do with prudence than right" (551–2).

[48] McClure, 233–4, 237–8. Nacol similarly references the "felt experience of oppression" (588). See also Grant, 179; Myers, 225; Casson, 251–2.

What may be most interesting because it is least evident, the majority may be moved to action when it feels a threat to the laws—to "their laws" (*2T* 209). Here we may see the effect of Locke's constitutional language on public opinion, in the extension of the concept of property rights to the laws themselves and thus to a felt sense of ownership of the law or constitution itself.[49] Such judgment is likely to arrive too late (*2T* 220). Only a "long train of Abuses, Prevarications, and Artifices...make[s] the design visible" so that the people may see and feel the problem (*2T* 225). The public is inattentive to the nuances of constitutionalism.[50] But the majority may sometimes be moved as well "if the mischief and oppression has lighted on some few"—that is, on "some private men's cases" (*2T* 208–209). The private case will interest the public if it seems to establish a precedent ("a long train of actings"; *2T* 210) for broader abuse that could "threaten all."[51] Locke does not counsel waiting for the long train to become visible. To do so is "to bid them first to be Slaves, and then to take care of their Liberty" (*2T* 220). The public response will arrive too late unless the public, or some members of it, are sufficiently vigilant to act before the train is visible.[52]

Not everyone will experience a sense of ownership of the laws. In this context it is helpful to consider Locke's distinction between tacit consent (which includes merely traveling through a territory) and express consent (which includes an attitude of membership; *2T* 121).[53] Express consent makes any person "a Perfect Member of

---

[49] In this I largely follow Myers, 191–5, and McClure, 234–8.

[50] Kleinerman, 215, 217. Myers suggests that the public's complacency—its disinclination to hotheadedness—may be a sign of its prudence or common sense (226).

[51] McClure expresses some doubt about the validity of moving from private experience to public judgments, and in particular whether Locke conflates the private need with a public good (268–72).

[52] Pangle, 254–8; Ward, 128; Corbett, 9.

[53] John W. Gough rejects the member-subject distinction in *John Locke's Political Philosophy: Eight Studies* (Oxford, Clarendon Press, 1973) 45, 65.

that Society" (*2T* 117). Locke suggests as well that there is a permanence to this attitude of membership; it establishes a "perpetual[] and indispensabl[e]" obligation (*2T* 121). In a short essay in the manuscripts of 1679 called "Amor Patriae," Locke describes this perpetual attitude of attachment. It is the attitude of one who maintains a "constant affection" for his homeland, even when he is traveling abroad, who wishes to bring home "improvements" and to win "esteem," and who most of all wants to live in a land where he is not a stranger and has no thought of departure.[54] Express consent is the felt sense of political obligation. In contrast to the one who only tacitly consents, the true member of society seems to have relinquished the option of exit in favor of loyalty and voice.

These members likely form an active minority within the public.[55] Yet Locke also suggests that if the members are an elite, it is an

---

Locke's distinction between express and tacit consent does not rest on a distinction of actions. Oaths may be signs of express consent and membership, but sometimes oaths are signs of tacit consent only (*2T*.116–7, 122). Property ownership may be a sign of express consent, but sometimes it is a sign of tacit consent (*2T*.119). Nor is there a difference with regard to the obligation under civil law (*2T*.119). Nor does there seem to be a clear distinction with regard to reason; some people may become members—which Locke associates with express consent—without even noticing it (*2T*.119). Rather than being defined by particular actions, or by a fully reasoned judgment, express consent is most closely related to a patriotic sentiment of attachment.

[54] Josephson, 147–60. In contrast, Scott argues that obligation is grounded on reason, not sentiment (547). Cf. John Dunn, *The Political Thought of John Locke: An Historical Account of the Argument of the Two Treatises of Government* (New York: Cambridge University press, 1969), 133–9. For "Amor Patriae" see *Political Essays*, Mark Goldie ed. (Cambridge: Cambridge University Press, 1997), 275.

[55] This conclusion is implied by Locke's account of prerogative as well. The prerogative power is founded on the "common law of nature" (*2T* 159). The exercise of prerogative seems to rest on the natural right to execute the law of nature. As an act of private will that carries no public authority, at least initially, it is like the act of "a single private Person" (*2T* 151). See Josephson, 240–1; Faulkner, 13; Corbett, 159; compare Ward,

elite with many points of access. Locke gestures toward these diverse motives. A minority of "a few oppressed Men" may be the first to draw attention to the violation of their rights. Other "private" and "factious" men are stirred by "a busie head or turbulent spirit," or by "Pride" and "Ambition," or by "Revenge" and "Covetousness" (*2T* 199, 208, 230). Even those moved by a desire to bring "improvements" also want to earn "esteem" ("Amor Patriae"). These are the ones who "will wish and seek for the opportunity" of political engagement (*2T* 224). While Locke expects that most folks will be generally complacent, politically, most of the time (and liberalism may foster a turn toward private affairs), he also seems to expect a politically active minority—patriots and scoundrels motivated by a wide range of desires including desires for liberty and dominion—to engage in frequent political contestation.

Conclusion

Locke offers a quiet but robust account of the character of liberal political life. At the beginning of the book, Locke points to the problem of political authority, but he does not resolve the problem through a theory of sovereign power. It may be a hallmark of liberalism that the normative terms of the debate do not finally settle the political debate. In a regime oriented around a concept of socio-political liberty, the question of political authority is bound to remain a little bit unsettled. And yet the regime, the liberal way of life, has its own authority; at least it hedges us in from bogs and precipices. It has a character, and its members have a character too. It is a regime that fosters certain

---

107. Fatovic also sees that prerogative is derived from a natural power but does not draw the conclusion that it is therefore available to political actors other than the executive (286ff). Leonard C. Feldman argues against the hypothesis of elite cueing in Locke's political community, and in favor of a broader practice in which something approaching the entire public acts as political judge. See Feldman's "Judging Necessity: Democracy and Extralegalism," *Political Theory*, vol. 36 No. 4 (August 2008): 550–577. I argue that Locke conceives of different levels of engagement in public life. There is a political elite that cues a broader public; the question is who might constitute that elite.

traits or habits (toleration, attention to private and worldly affairs, a concern for popular opinion and esteem) while sublimating others (zealotry, learning, claims of extraordinary virtue and superiority).

And it is recognizably political in that it shares in the character or nature of political life generally. The Lockean liberal regime includes flavors of Machiavellian tumult and Madisonian faction. It is a regime framed by a political concept of individual liberty and rights the exercise of which is subject to public or majoritarian judgment. The exercise of political power will be contested not only by well-reasoned people but by turbulent and ambitious private men as well. Instead of a legal or juridical test, a mathematical standard for measuring tyranny, Locke leaves the public with the right to judge by means of its affective response—its sensed experience of politics. If there is to be a public judgment (and not merely a collection of individual judgments) then it seems such judgment is political, not philosophical.

In the end Locke gives us a markedly *political* theory. He offers a liberal response to the intrinsic problems of political life: of the contest between the demands of right and justice and the practical necessities of the exercise of power; of the interplay of nature, history, and convention, and of reason, passion, and custom; of the shaping of a public and a public character, and the ordering of a regime; and especially of the perpetual and irresolvable contest between private and public goods. Throughout, Locke weaves together the normative and the prudential, theory and practice. The very structure of his presentations—his typical rhetorical method of beginning with a normative claim only to complicate the presentation with considerations of political reality—points to this concern. When we see that Locke's liberalism is part of the recognizable political landscape, and think of the liberal regime as a way of political living, we can better make our own judgment about the goodness of such a regime in comparison to the alternatives.

2.

JOHN LOCKE'S RELIGIOUS TOLERATION: THE ANNAPOLIS MANUSCRIPT

Steven Forde

John Locke is the father of religious toleration—that is the way he is known to many. Locke was certainly not the first to champion toleration, but his arguments were powerfully influential in the development of religious and political thought and action in his own century and beyond. He shaped the thinking of the eighteenth-century Enlightenment, and in particular the American Founding Fathers. Locke's religious toleration is, to a significant degree, our religious toleration.

Yet some interpreters today are given pause by aspects of Locke's doctrine of toleration. Particularly questionable, in their eyes, are his refusal to extend toleration to atheists (if that qualifies as "religious intolerance"), and his ambivalence toward tolerating Catholics. Locke's attitude toward atheists is conditioned by the theology and psychology outlined at length in his premier philosophical work, the *Essay Concerning Human Understanding*.[1] By those arguments, rewards and punishments after death are necessary to make it rational for human beings to obey moral law when it is not in their interest or does not contribute to their happiness.[2] Atheists, who necessarily disbelieve in such rewards and punish-

---

[1] John Locke, *An Essay Concerning Human Understanding* (Amherst, New York: Prometheus Books, 1995 [1689]). For a review of the controversy on Locke's toleration, see Adam Wolfson, "Toleration and Relativism: The Locke-Proast Exchange," *The Review Of Politics* 59:2 (spring 1997): 213–231.

[2] At least, this is the argument I have made elsewhere: Steven Forde, *Locke, Science, and Politics* (Cambridge: Cambridge University Press, 2013) especially Chapter 2.

ments, lack the essential motivation to be reliably moral. As to his attitude toward Catholicism, it evolved over the course of his career, as we shall see.

Locke's attitude toward Catholicism, and his philosophy of toleration in general, changed significantly over time. In his early *Tracts on Government*, Locke adopts a largely Hobbesian stance on politics, which includes ceding power over religion, at least in its outward manifestations, to the sovereign.[3] These were written in 1660 and 1662. By 1667 Locke had come around to a much more tolerant view, as we see in his *Essay on Toleration*, drafted in that year. We will have occasion to look more closely at this essay, as it is essentially contemporaneous with the manuscript that is our central focus. Suffice it to say for now that Locke in the *Essay* rehearses some of his more famous mature arguments for general toleration, while denying that toleration to Catholics. Finally, Locke published his more famous *Letter Concerning Toleration* in 1689,[4] the final statement that guided the tolerationist movement for centuries afterward. Yet even here, there is doubt as to how far toleration of Catholics is intended.

Whether we agree or disagree with the particulars of Locke's argument, we can learn from the evolution of his thought. The path that led him from quasi-Hobbesianism to toleration and what became known as the "separation of church and state" is a path that devotees of toleration might wish the intolerant of today to follow. That path is worth tracing out. Even from Locke's hesitancy regarding Catholics we can draw reflections on the question of where the limits of toleration lie, and why. Today, in an age when religious intolerance has become a newly urgent issue, it is worth examining the experience and thought of one of the pioneers of tolerance.

---

[3] Locke, *First Tract on Government, Second Tract on Government* (from 1660 and c.1662, respectively). In Locke, *Political Essays*, Mark Goldie, ed. (Cambridge: Cambridge University Press) 3-78.

[4] *A Letter Concerning Toleration*, trans William Popple, ed. James H. Tully (Indianapolis: Hackett, 1983). Hereafter cited as *LT* by page number.

_____

In 2015, a lost manuscript of Locke was discovered at the Green-field Library at St. John's College in Annapolis, Maryland, a discovery not widely publicized until 2019.[5] It is brief, only about 1000 words long. Its first page bears the heading *Reasons for tolerating Papists equally with others*. The Annapolis Manuscript (as I will call it) bears the endorsement "Toleration 67" in Locke's hand, indicating it seems the date of composition. It consists of a series of bullet points recording Locke's reactions to a pamphlet published at that time by one Charles Wolseley,[6] and it contains the first version of some of the language contained in Locke's *Essay on Toleration*, written around the same time.[7] Part of its interest is the light it sheds on Locke's thinking regarding the proper limits of toleration as he moved toward a more expansive understanding of toleration. Catholicism provided the foil for these reflections. The bullet points of Locke's manuscript are keyed to page numbers in Wolseley's pamphlet, and respond to specific points made on those pages.

Wolseley's pamphlet argues for extending toleration to all Protestants, including dissenters or non-conformists. It does not propose extending toleration to Catholics. Wolseley does not make

_____

[5] See Walmsley, J. C. and Felix Waldmann, "John Locke and the Toleration of Catholics: A New Manuscript," *The Historical Journal* 62:4 (2019): 1093–1115. It is somewhat misleading to call this a "lost" manuscript, as it was publicly auctioned several times in the early twentieth century (as part of bundles of manuscripts) and was duly registered on each occasion. Its significance, however, was not recognized until recently. See Walmsley and Waldmann, 1195–96.

[6] "Liberty of Conscience, The Magistrates Interest: or, To grant *Liberty of Conscience* to Persons of different perswasions in matters of Religion, is the great Interest of all Kingdoms and States, and particularly of ENG-LAND; *Asserted* and *Proved*." London, 1668. I will cite this as "Magistrate's Interest."

[7] Locke never published the *Essay on Toleration*, which exists in different drafts. The accepted date for the earliest of these drafts is 1667. See Locke, *Political Essays*, p. 134. For more on the dating of the manuscript, its background and history, see Walmsley and Waldmann, 1094–1103.

a theme of this, barely mentioning it in fact.[8] He presumes that his English audience takes it for granted that toleration should not be extended to Catholics. Locke's Annapolis Manuscript focuses on toleration of Catholicism exclusively, indicating the issue was foremost in his mind at this point. Wolseley, in the body of his pamphlet, makes a number of arguments for toleration that might be thought to apply to Catholics; for the most part, Locke presents arguments as to why Wolseley's tolerationist arguments should not be extended to Catholics. Despite the overall thrust of the Annapolis Manuscript being against toleration of Catholics, its tone has been described as "emollient."[9] As we shall see, some of Locke's arguments do point in the direction of toleration for Catholics, and even those that turn against Catholicism appeal to reason rather than invective. Before we explore Locke's views, however, we should take a brief view of the state of toleration in the England of Locke's day, the milieu into which he was injecting his writings on toleration.

The immediate period of the Annapolis Manuscript, 1667–8, saw a surge of pamphlets on toleration, some twenty-three or more. Wolseley's pamphlet was among these. Parliament was in session, the monarchy had been weakened for reasons unrelated to toleration, and non-conforming Protestants were agitating for greater toleration.[10] Wolseley, who identified himself on the title page only as "a Protestant, a lover of Peace, and the Prosperity of the Nation," was among those arguing for a universal toleration of Protestants. In 1662, in the aftermath of the Civil War and the Cromwellian Protectorate (when Puritans had altered much church law and practice), the Church of England had sponsored an Act of Uniformity, man-

---

[8] See for example Wolseley, "Magistrate's Interest," p. 14. Wolseley gives a short précis of reasons Catholics are not eligible for toleration.

[9] Walmsley and Waldmann, 1102.

[10] See Walmsley and Waldmann, 1094–5, and John Coffey, *Persecution and toleration in Protestant England, 1558-1689* (Harlow, 2000) 166–79.

dating conformity to the Church's *Book of Common Prayer* in public prayers, sacraments, and other rites. Conformity was required to hold any office in Church or government, a requirement that did not sit well with Protestants who objected to elements of the practice thus established. Thus was "non-conformity" born. More than 2,000 clergy of the Church of England itself refused to take the oath stipulated by the Act and were expelled from the Church. Further Acts forbade non-conforming meetings for worship (the Conventicle Act), and barred non-conforming clergy from coming within five miles of any incorporated town, or teaching in schools (the Five-Mile Act).[11] This regime of non-conformist persecution was the target of dissenters in the changed political landscape of 1667–8. Although they had little success until the Toleration Act of 1688 (which itself was only a very qualified success), their agitation spawned new writing and (in the case of Locke at least) new thinking about toleration.

The position of Catholics in law was worse than that of the non-conforming Protestants, naturally enough, but the picture is somewhat more nuanced than this suggests. The king throughout this period, Charles II, though head of the Church of England, had definite sympathies with Catholicism. His mother was a Catholic, and he married a Catholic. His brother, who ascended the throne in 1685 as James II, was Catholic himself. James's ascension was not blocked, giving England an overtly Catholic king.[12] Charles, on royal prerogative, promulgated a "Declaration of Indulgence" in 1662 that, remarkably, decreed toleration for Catholics as well as Protestants. He hoped to put Catholic and Protestant on more equal ground with this unilateral move. The ploy backfired badly— Parliament revoked the decree at the earliest opportunity and replaced it with the oppressive Acts mentioned above—but it does

---

[11] Other acts during this period that mandated religious uniformity included the Test Act of 1673 and the Corporation Act of 1661.

[12] This is not to say there was no opposition to it. When James II had a son and Catholic heir apparent, Protestants rebelled, forced James's abdication, and brought in the Protestant William and Mary in the "Glorious Revolution" of 1688.

show that England did not speak with an entirely unified voice on the subject of Catholic toleration. There was even a Tory faction that supported indulgence for Catholics. The stirrings of tolerance for Catholics in the halls of power, however, aroused grave suspicions in other quarters. There was a longstanding fear that Charles secretly designed to return England to the Catholic fold. This suspicion, it turns out, had justification. In 1670, Charles concluded a secret pact with Louis XIV of France to make England Catholic at a suitable opportunity, with armed French assistance if necessary. Secret though it was, some hints of this "Treaty of Dover" leaked out, reinforcing Protestant fears that a return to Catholicism would mean English subordination to a foreign prince. In the event, meaningful relief from persecution for Catholics did not come to England until the late eighteenth and early nineteenth century, more than one hundred years later.

It is noteworthy that Locke, in the Annapolis Manuscript, is responding to only one of two pamphlets that Charles Wolseley produced in the flurry of pamphleteering that year. The two are companion pieces and were published nearly simultaneously. The one Locke is responding to is the second. In the first, whose title is even more cumbersome than that of the pamphlet drawing Locke's interest,[13] Wolseley focused on the magistrate's duties of *conscience* in the matter of toleration. The piece Locke responds to deals with the magistrate's *interest* in toleration, that is, considerations of national interest apart from any duties of conscience. This is appropriate, as the Annapolis Manuscript accentuates the fact that Locke's arguments against the toleration of Catholics have not to do with Catholic *doctrine* (except insofar as it might lead directly to actions endangering the public), but only with questions of whether Catho-

---

[13] It is "Liberty of Conscience, Upon its true and proper Grounds Asserted & Vindicated, proving That no Prince, nor State, ought by force to compel Men to any part of the Doctrine, Worship, or Discipline of the Gospel. Written by a Protestant, a lover of Truth, and the Peace and Prosperity of the Nation."

lics will have allegiances contrary to their duties as citizens, and hence are likely to *act* in ways that undermine the polity.

As noted, the first page of the Annapolis Manuscript bears the heading "Reasons for tolerating Papists equally with others," and itemizes, by page, those of Wolseley's arguments that in Locke's view present valid reasons for tolerating Catholics (even though that was not Wolseley's aim). The remaining three pages of the manuscript bear no separate heading but could be entitled "Reasons for *not* tolerating Papists equally with others." Locke begins again from the start of Wolseley's pamphlet, with bullet points keyed to the relevant pages in Wolseley. He considers other of Wolseley's arguments that one might take to apply to Catholics, treating them now with great skepticism. One singularity of the Wolseley pamphlet is that it often makes such blanket defenses of toleration that a reader might be excused for assuming they are meant to apply to Catholics as well as Protestants. He states, for example, that persecuting subjects for mere religion will necessarily "disgust" them, while freedom will "oblige;" men will naturally "love that Prince or State, where they find favour and protection" (*Magistrate's Interest*, p. 4). Moreover, onlookers will have a natural sympathy with the persecuted (pp. 5, 6). Near the end of the pamphlet, Wolseley argues that it is the interest of the king to use the services of all his subjects, rather than excluding some on the basis of religious opinion. He even instances the King of France, where Protestant and Catholic were indeed both tolerated at the time and employed in the public service (p. 17).

Locke's responses to these arguments in the Annapolis Manuscript sometimes accept them as arguments in favor of tolerating Catholics, though for the most part his responses detail reasons why these tolerationist arguments should not be extended to Catholics. To begin with, as noted, the opening page of the Manuscript is devoted to reasons in favor of toleration. Here, for example, Locke writes "Persecution disobliges the best sort amongst the papists as well as amongst others," extending an argument Wolseley made on page 7 of his pamphlet. Similarly, Locke accepts that "If all subjects should be equally countenanced & employed by the prince, the papists have an equal title" (referencing Wolseley p. 17), and "If to force dissenters to one's opinion be contrary to the rule of religion & to no purpose, papists should be tolerated" (re: p. 18). Wolseley made these arguments but did not extend them to Catholics; Locke extends them. On the other hand, some of Locke's "Reasons for tolerating Papists equally with others" paradoxically cut against Catholics. These include "If liberty of conscience make all men daily more & more to abhor popery papists may be tolerated as well as others" (re: p. 12). That is, toleration of Catholics is acceptable if it is the best way to promote hostility to Catholics. Similarly, "If liberty of conscience unite the protestants against the papists, papists may safely be tolerated" (re: p. 13) and "If toleration be the way to convert papists as well as others, they may equally be tolerated" (re: p. 15).

The majority of the Annapolis Manuscript is devoted to reasons why Wolseley's arguments for universal Protestant toleration might not be extended to Catholics. Where Wolseley argued that intolerance only begets sympathy to those being persecuted, an argument that *prima facie* would apply to Catholics, Locke rejoins, "Standers-by will be less dissatisfied with severity used to papists than to others because it is lex talionis." This is based on the notion that Catholics are intolerant to Protestants in their home countries (the example of France notwithstanding), and so do not merit toleration in Protestant countries—or at least that the resident Protestants would not see it that way. Wolseley argued on behalf of non-conforming Protestants that, if they are factious against the state, it is persecution that made them so; they are in fact being persecuted for conscience, not faction (p. 4). Locke argues that this does not apply to Catholics since "those who are absolutely disposed of by an authority supposed infallible, whose interest is directly opposite to yours, must necessarily be all factious however some of them may be sincerely conscientious." Their allegiance to a supposed infallible foreign leader makes even (precisely!) conscientious Catholics factious in any Protestant state. In such a case, it is the interest of the king to suppress Catholicism, not for its doctrines, but for its politically subversive nature. Near the end of the Annapolis Manuscript, Locke puts the case this way:

> I doubt whether upon protestant principles we can justify
> punishing of papists for their speculative opinions, as pur-
> gatory [or] transubstantiation if they stopped there. But
> possibly no reason nor religion obliges us to tolerate those
> whose practical principles necessarily lead them to the ea-
> ger persecution of all opinions & the utter destruction of
> all societies but their own, so that it is not the difference
> of their opinion in religion, or of their ceremonies in wor-
> ship, but their dangerous & factious tenets in reference to
> the state (which are blended with & make a part of their
> religion) that exclude them from the benefit of toleration.
> (re: Wolseley, p. 11)

As we shall see, this is the position Locke adopted in the *Essay
on Toleration*, written the same year. Note that it is emphatically not
the "speculative opinions" of Catholics (and Locke here pointedly
lists two doctrines that many Protestants considered to be unacceptable), but the political consequences of some of their doctrines,
that exclude them from toleration. Not the magistrate's conscience,
to use Wolseley's terminology, but the magistrate's interest dictates
the choice.

Aside from instances like this, where the published *Essay on
Toleration* demonstrates that some of the arguments formulated in
the Annapolis Manuscript were indeed adopted by Locke, it is difficult to gauge the exact purport of the exercise Locke undertakes in
the manuscript. Was Locke making these arguments sincerely and
in his own name? Was he playing devil's advocate, using Wolseley
as a foil just to clarify his own thinking? Was he preparing a polemic
against Wolseley? Absent some new evidence, perhaps from another
still-undiscovered manuscript, we may never know. Given that the
Manuscript advances arguments that cut opposite ways, it seems
most likely that Locke was using this occasion to sort out his own
thinking. Our interest in the matter, however, is not to establish the
biographical or historical details per se but to learn something about
the evolution of Locke's thinking on toleration, and by extension

the evolution that others may take in the same direction.

The first major expression we have of Locke's thinking on religious toleration is two *Tracts on Government*, the first published in 1660 and the second in 1662.[14] As previously mentioned, these *Tracts* take a remarkably Hobbesian stance on politics. Locke professes to be indifferent as to whether government is rooted in paternal power or consent of the governed—on that score, he sides with neither Filmer nor Hobbes—but in either case, sovereign power must be absolute, for that is the only way that peace may be maintained (pp. 9–12, 70–71). That is, if government is rooted in a social contract, citizens must transfer all of their right for government to be secure.

Like Hobbes, Locke blames English writers for the bloodshed and chaos of the English Civil War.[15] Though Locke professes love for liberty, he maintains that turbulent authors' championing of liberty undermined the crucial pillar of authority. Much of the rancor that fueled this conflict was religiously inspired, from which both Hobbes and the Locke of the *Tracts* concluded that religious uniformity, established by law, was the only way to secure peace in a nation. The "liberty" contended for by the advocates of complete freedom of worship, Locke writes, would merely unleash a "tyranny of religious rage," turning every sect into a zealot's crusade against religious practice and belief differing from their own (pp. 7, 40). Based on the experience of the Civil War and its aftermath in the Puritan Commonwealth, this was not a completely unreasonable fear. It haunts the whole of Locke's thinking about toleration, at the time of the *Tracts* and afterward.

Discussions of toleration in Locke's day revolved in part around

---

[14] Mark Goldie, ed., *Locke: Political Essays* (Cambridge: Cambridge University Press, 1997), 3–78. Future citations in this section will be given by page numbers in the text.

[15] *Tracts*, p. 5; *cf.* Hobbes *Leviathan* (ed. Edwin Curley, Indianapolis: Hackett, 1994) ch. 29, 30 et al.

the concept of "matters indifferent" or "things indifferent."[16] In religious terms, matters indifferent included rituals and practices that were not grounded in authoritative religious sources, primarily Scripture, but were characteristic of a particular denomination by custom. These would include the time and place of worship, whether believers stand or kneel when they pray, what kind of vestments are worn by the clergy, the details of liturgy, or the mode of internal church governance.[17] Locke takes the view, also espoused by the Church of England,[18] that all such customs are indifferent in the sense that they are not commanded by God, though they may be instituted as part of the communion of any group of believers. According to Locke, God accepts worship in any of these forms, so long as it is sincere (p. 29). Still, in the *Tracts* he supports state-mandated uniformity in these forms and manners, lest conflict or even war result from sectarians seeking to impose their rite on all. This is the paradox of the position Locke (along with a great many of his countrymen) adopts: these matters are religiously indifferent, virtually irrelevant in God's eyes, but must be controlled because they occasion fanaticism in believers, each for his own sect.

Locke's argument for this position in the *Tracts* is both theological and political. He begins by expanding the notion of "matters indifferent" beyond the ecclesiastical realm. Natural law (which is also divine law, being established by God) places certain restrictions on mankind. Much law promulgated by human sovereigns essentially recapitulates or makes explicit the natural law that is binding apart from the human sovereign's will. But there is a wide swath of

---

[16] The terminology derives from the Greek word *adiaphora* (a word that appeared in the debates of Locke's time), meaning "making no difference."

[17] The importance of the last is indicated by the very names adopted by many denominations. Presbyterian, Episcopalian, and Congregationalist all refer to modes of church governance.

[18] The Preface to the 1662 edition of the *Book of Common Prayer* acknowledged that "the particular Forms of Divine Worship, and the Rites and Ceremonies appointed to be used therein" were "things in their own nature indifferent, and alterable."

human activity unaddressed by divine or natural law. These for Locke are all "matters indifferent" in the wider sense (pp. 76–77). The human magistrate, he argues, has complete power to regulate matters unaddressed by divine or natural law (p. 67). These would include such things as establishing a common currency, or rules of judicial procedure, or regulations of trade and traffic. Here, the obligation of subjects derives not from the binding power of natural law directly, but indirectly from the natural-law mandate that political authority be created and obeyed (pp. 64, 66). Thus we get the absolutism of the *Tracts*, but we should note as well that it allows Locke to bring the discussion of religious "matters indifferent" under the umbrella of matters indifferent per se. His argument is essentially that religious "matters indifferent" are to be treated no differently than those that are more mundane, such as regulations of commerce. To sectarians who would carve out an exception for "freedom of conscience," excluding the magistrate from regulating religious practice, Locke replies that such an argument would destroy the magistrate's authority over all matters indifferent, rendering civil government impossible (p. 77).

The validity of this argument is open to question. In addition, the very existence of such sectarians exposes a difficulty in Locke's position. They refuse to accept the magistrate's authority over their rituals, believing their practices mandated by God. Yet Locke (apparently) hopes to persuade them on the grounds that their rituals are "indifferent" in the eyes of God, an argument they have already rejected. Their zeal is fueled precisely by the notion that it would be an affront to God to practice Anglican ritual (for example) simply because the human magistrate has mandated it (p. 42). The difficulty is only magnified when we see that Locke resigns himself to the fact that uniformity of religious belief cannot be expected or imposed. Requiring uniform belief, of course, would be the best means to social concord, if it were possible. European history since the Reformation, however, demonstrates such uniformity to be forever beyond reach, as Locke acknowledges (p. 14). But the same history—in particular the history of religious strife in England during Locke's time—might have persuaded an observer that uniformity of *ritual* is equally unattainable by magisterial fiat. Locke carves out a theologically defensible position, yielding the policy prescription that ritual be made uniform, while belief be left free in the privacy of individual conscience (pp. 13, 14, 58). As Locke himself later realized, however, this is not a viable position in practice.

This brings us back to the Annapolis Manuscript and the *Essay on Toleration* of 1667, which reflects its influence.[19] These represent a mid-point in the evolution of Locke's thinking on toleration, in some respects a real change from the position of the *Tracts*. To begin with, Locke now acknowledges that practice and belief should not and cannot be separated in the way that the *Tracts* had hoped. Toleration must be extended to "things indifferent" in religious practice, unless the practices in question are clearly destructive to society (p. 140). For "in religious worship nothing is indifferent," that is, believers are typically convinced that their rituals are not indifferent and cannot be persuaded otherwise (p. 139). He explicitly repudiates the argument of the *Tracts* to the effect that carving out an exception for religious practice will annihilate the magistrate's power over all indifferent matters. In the *Essay*, two arguments converge to produce this shift. First is the argument that "a man cannot command his own understanding" (p. 137). This is a position Locke adhered to for the rest of his life. It is key to the argument of the *Letter Concerning Toleration* of 1689 and justified at length in the *Essay Concerning Human Understanding,* Locke's definitive account of epistemology and mind. It does not mean that men's minds cannot be changed by persuasion or new evidence; it simply means that *command*—even self-command—has no effect on the process (p. 142). I cannot change beliefs simply by wanting to change beliefs, and no command from outside is capable of doing so either. Hence legal mandates of the type used in religious regulation are ineffective as well as oppressive. The second major change this reveals in

---

[19] A side-by-side comparison of the two works, showing the influence, is produced by Walmsley and Waldmann, 1103–1111.

Locke's view is more practical. Locke was quite certain in the *Tracts* that allowing diversity of practice would lead religious people inexorably into conflict, even war. The freshness of the experience of civil war and its aftermath in 1660 and 1662 doubtless made this fear more plausible, but Locke by 1667 evidently had decided that diversity of practice could coexist with peace and concord. Locke's recently inaugurated relationship with Anthony Ashley Cooper, the first earl of Shaftesbury, a tolerationist political figure, is often given partial credit for changing Locke's views.[20] The experience of nations where toleration was allowed was likely also pivotal in this shift.

Locke's new position in the *Essay* is supported as well by a third change in Locke's thinking, a change in some ways deeper than the first two. It pertains not simply to religious issues but to the foundations of political philosophy. This is a principled justification for strict limits on the magistrate's power. Though Locke in the *Essay* is not yet willing to pronounce unambiguously for consent and a social contract as the basis of the magistrate's authority, he does assert the purpose of this authority to be limited to the preservation of the citizens and the concerns of this life (p. 136). Whereas in the *Tracts* he had started with consent (or paternal authority, it did not matter) to arrive at absolutism, we can glimpse in the *Essay* the argument Locke will develop at length in the *Two Treatises of Government* concerning the logic of consent. By this logic, the existence of consent at the origin of government allows us to conclude that citizens will not have given more power to the magistrate than absolutely necessary to the fulfillment of his charge. This rests on the suppositions that citizen-contractors are rationally self-interested, that they prize their liberty, and that government does not need absolute power to do its job. Thus, if tolerating a range of religious practices will not erupt in social conflict and violence, the power to regulate such practices must never have been given to the

---

[20] See, *e.g.*, Richard Ashcraft, *Revolutionary Politics & Locke's Two Treatises of Government* (Princeton: Princeton University Press, 1986), 80–84; Walmsley and Waldmann, 1094.

government in the first place.

This is not to say that the *Essay* foreshadows the *Second Treatise of Government* in all respects. Though Locke allows more or less unfettered liberty of religious practice—to the extent of allowing disobedience of any laws that contravene it (p. 140)—the magistrate has sole authority to determine what laws serve the public good in this area (p. 142). This is true moreover in all spheres of the magistrate's purview: "he is not accountable to any tribunal here," Locke avers (p. 142). Citizens who violate such laws, even if illegitimate because they overstep the magistrate's power, must accept the punishment, as they are not allowed to second-guess the magistrate (p. 143). In particular, "conscience" entitles no one to disobey the law (p. 140). Similarly, though private conscience is beyond his reach, the magistrate can and should prevent the publication of any opinions or doctrines that in his view threaten public peace and order, however conscientiously held (p. 141).

Toward the end of the *Essay on Toleration*, Locke abruptly changes theme. In an echo of Charles Wolseley's procedure of writing separately on the magistrate's duties of conscience in toleration, and what his interest prompts, Locke launches a discussion of what the magistrate "ought to do in prudence" (p. 151). This section, and thus the *Essay* as a whole, is unfinished, but it is in this section more than any other that Locke makes use of arguments developed in the Annapolis Manuscript, that is, arguments as to why withholding toleration from Catholicism will not have the negative consequences that suppressing dissenting or non-conforming Protestants would have, in the case of England at least. Here, Locke says, the only question is "whether toleration or imposition be the readiest way to secure the safety and peace, and promote the welfare, of this kingdom?" In the case of Protestants, prudence dictates toleration because oppression of dissenting sects will cause them to unite in opposition to the government and create sympathy in onlookers for their plight. Catholics, Locke asserts, can never unite with any Protestants, as no Protestants will unite with them, so oppressing them will never create a general party of opposition (p. 152). The premise is that a gulf divides Catholicism and Protestantism that will not be bridged. For the same reason, Protestant onlookers will not sympathize with oppressed Catholics. This is particularly so because, Locke says, Englishmen know that the Catholic Church practices intolerance toward Protestants wherever they are in power (p. 152)—the *lex talionis* clause of the Annapolis Manuscript.

The gravest charge Locke levels against Catholicism in the Annapolis Manuscript and the *Essay on Toleration*, though, concerns their political loyalties. He takes the position that Catholics have sworn a "blind obedience" to an "infallible pope," an allegiance that in their minds supersedes their allegiance to the English monarchy (p. 152). This is not a mere "speculative opinion," but a practical teaching. If the pope has designs to bring England back into the Catholic fold, and his followers are sworn to obey him over their secular rulers, they cannot but be subversive of peace and order in the realm, indeed in any realm where Catholicism is not already the established religion (p. 151). True, the ostensive power of the pope over secular affairs is but one of many Catholic doctrines, and we have already seen that Locke is fully willing to tolerate purely speculative doctrines such as transubstantiation or purgatory. Locke notes though that men generally embrace the doctrines of their sects "in a bundle," the good with the bad (p. 146). It is very difficult to get believers to separate the good from the bad in their religious creeds. Locke does not assert categorically that Catholics would not be able to undertake such a winnowing. He merely says that they "ought not to be tolerated by the magistrate…unless he can be secured that he can allow one part" of Catholic doctrine "without the spreading of the other," that the subversive parts of Catholic doctrine will not infect others (p. 146). Gaining such assurance, however, is "very hard to be done." Either way, this observation cements the proof that Locke's treatment of Catholics is dictated by practical and political considerations, rather than purely theological or speculative ones. As such, it could be overturned by a different estimate of the political consequences of Catholic doctrine, or of the ability of devout Catholics to shed part of their creed.

———

The *Letter Concerning Toleration* (with its ensuing polemics[21]) constitutes Locke's final statement on religious toleration, published in 1689. At the beginning of the *Letter*, Locke asserts that toleration is "the chief Characteristical Mark of the True Church."[22] It is the duty of all believers to embrace toleration, the duty of all clergy to preach it (*LT* p. 50), and the duty of the magistrate to practice it in his official capacity. Liberty of conscience is every man's natural right (*LT* p. 51). In religious doctrine and most of religious practice, there must be a strict separation between what we have come to call "church" and "state" (*LT cf.* p. 33). These duties are rooted in the notions that coercion can have no effect on inner belief, and that "the Business of True Religion" is "the regulating Mens Lives according to the Rules of Vertue and Piety," rather than, for example, elaborating rituals or speculative doctrines. These notions are familiar to us from Locke's earlier writings. Familiar too is the claim he makes here that, when a law is framed legitimately to serve the public good, it prevails over all claims of conscience. In the *Letter*, Locke still maintains that any religious practices that contravene such a law must give way to the magistrate's authority (*LT* pp. 42, 48).

Some present-day followers of Locke—citizens in modern, liberal societies—have qualms about the absolute priority Locke gives to civil authority over conscience in such cases. What causes the greatest unease, however, are the limitations he puts on toleration itself. He would not extend toleration to atheists, for example, a

---

[21] In response to critics (primarily the Anglican Jonas Proast), Locke wrote *A Second Letter Concerning Toleration* (*The Works of John Locke*, vol. 5, London: Routledge/Thoemmes, 1997, pp. 59–137); *A Third Letter for Toleration*. (*The Works of John Locke*, vol. 5. London: Routledge/Thoemmes, 1997, pp. 141–546); and *A Fourth Letter for Toleration* (*The Works of John Locke*, vol. 5. London: Routledge/Thoemmes, 1997, pp. 549–574). Of these, the *Third Letter* is some 400 pages long, in ten chapters.

[22] *A Letter Concerning Toleration*, trans William Popple, ed. James H. Tully (Indianapolis: Hackett 1983), 23. Henceforth, citations to this work, *LT*, will be given parenthetically, by page number in the text.

stricture motivated, as we noted above, by Locke's notion that rewards and punishments in the next life are a necessary prop to human morality in this.[23] And, it is not entirely clear whether Locke
extends toleration to Catholics in the *Letter*, which is the question
of greatest interest to us. Given the amount of ink that has been
spilled in discussions of this issue,[24] I can do no more than give a
synopsis of the difficulties, and what light the Annapolis Manuscript might shed upon the matter.

It is true that Locke unleashes no diatribe against Catholics or
Catholicism in the *Letter*, as he had in the Annapolis Manuscript
and the *Essay* of 1667. He says some things that seem to point to
their toleration. He asserts, for example, that all Christians are in
agreement on "the Substantial and truly Fundamental part of Religion" (*LT* p. 36; 57). That part would be the very limited set of beliefs, mostly directed to morality and virtue, that are derived directly
and unequivocally from scripture. Locke is aware that many if not
most Christian denominations add extraneous articles to this core,
all of which are imbibed "in a bundle" by their congregants. This is
unavoidable; it is the source of the diversity of opinions that has so
unsettled the Christian world. It is also for the most part innocuous,
dealing with "matters indifferent," church ritual, governance, and so
on. So long as these congregants tolerate others who arrange things
differently, Locke has no objection to them. If any denomination
should insist upon rules or rituals—or doctrines—subversive of public order, however, Locke is clear, as he was in his earlier writings,
they are not to be tolerated. This was where his strictures against
Catholicism came from in the earlier writings. The *Letter* is somewhat ambiguous on the score of Catholicism. It does repeat some of
the arguments Locke used earlier against Catholicism, without explicitly linking them to Catholicism. He says for example the doctrine that "*Dominion is founded in Grace*" is utterly destructive of all

---

[23] p. 51. Of course, this ban would logically extend to theists who do
not believe in an afterlife, or a rewarding and punishing god. Some ver-
sions of Deism would fall in this category.

[24] See for example the array of works cited in Wolfson, "Toleration
and Relativism."

peace and security, or even "Common Friendship" (*LT* p. 33). This charge is here leveled at any Christians who seek political power for their denomination, but it was a charge leveled specifically against Catholics in Locke's earlier writings, due to the history of Popes claiming authority over the secular powers. Locke further singles out doctrines that "*Faith is not to be kept with Hereticks,*" that "*Kings excommunicated forfeit their Crowns and Kingdoms,*" or that denominations other than one's own are not to be tolerated, as poison to the commonwealth, and having no right to toleration (*LT* p. 50). Once again, Locke does not link Catholicism specifically to these doctrines here, though this linkage was partially the basis for his earlier anathemas against it. He also warns against any church that places believers under the service of another prince, a principal charge against Catholicism in the earlier writings. When Locke makes statements such as this in the *Letter*, one almost expects him to use them as arguments against tolerating Catholics, as he did in the earlier writings. Here, though, he instances only Muslims, or "Mahumetans," who cannot be good subjects, he says, so long as they pledge "blind obedience to the *Mufti* of *Constantinople*" (*LT* p. 50).

It is striking, therefore, when, only a few pages later, Locke pronounces that "neither *Pagan*, nor *Mahumetan*, nor *Jew*, ought to be excluded from the Civil Rights of the Commonwealth, because of his Religion" (*LT* p. 54). This directs our attention to a loophole in his apparent condemnation of Islam: it is conditional, applying only "so long as" Muslims have a duty of blind obedience to the Mufti of Constantinople. Locke is clearly entertaining the possibility that Muslims do not in fact feel any such duty, regardless of what the traditions of their religion may hold. Thus, their case is parallel to that of Catholics, about whom Locke's statements seem always to have been conditional in the same way. In the *Essay on Toleration*, we recall, Locke said Catholics could be tolerated so long as the magistrate could be absolutely assured that they do not have that kind of fealty to the Pope (*Essay*, p. 146). He there expressed great skepticism that Catholics could separate the noxious part of their doctrine from the innocuous. Has Locke changed his mind by the time of the *Letter Concerning Toleration*, some twenty years later?

The years he spent in exile in Holland, where he observed the peace and concord that religious toleration could bring, might have enlightened him about this too. Even if it did, though, Locke is clearly ambivalent about the issue. In the *Letter*, he uses Islam rather than Catholicism to remind us of what he formerly regarded as several of the biggest political problems with Catholicism. If he no longer connects these charges openly to Catholicism, he does not explicitly exonerate it either, leaving Catholicism potentially under a shadow. What is his view of this problem at the time of the *Letter*? And how much of a real shift in his position does it represent?

I would venture the hypothesis that the fundamentals of his position have not shifted significantly between the period of the Annapolis Manuscript and that of the *Letter Concerning Toleration*. His rejection of toleration for such doctrines as fealty to a foreign prince, belief that the Church may declare the secular prince a heretic and release citizens of all allegiance to the secular crown, that believers should be intolerant, that promises with heretics need not be kept— Locke consistently argues that any religion or denomination that adheres to such beliefs forfeits all entitlement to toleration. This is part of his position that civil law, when operating within its proper limits, has absolute supremacy over claims of "conscience." I would propose that what has changed between the *Essay on Toleration* and the *Letter Concerning Toleration* is his estimate of what Catholicism (and Islam) actually represent in practice. Both religions have, as part of their traditions, an unacceptable mixing of church and state, an absolutist hierarchical structure purportedly dating from the founding of their religions, and both are traditionally given to intolerance of other sects or religions. Locke was, at least from the time of the Annapolis Manuscript and the *Essay on Toleration*, perfectly tolerant of Catholicism, so far as its speculative doctrines and its practices in matters indifferent are concerned. At the same time, he was thoroughly convinced that Catholics, by their faith, are pledged to noxious practical doctrines, though he was willing to entertain the (slim) possibility that they could "unbundle" those beliefs from the innocuous portion of their creed (*Essay*, p. 146). In the *Letter*, Locke repeats his anathema against the practical doctrines subversive of political order, but now conspicuously refrains from linking them to Catholicism. He also conspicuously refrains from exonerating Catholicism of these charges in any explicit way. This is why debates persist about Locke's ultimate attitude toward the Church of Rome. The conclusion I am drawing is that Locke is now willing, perhaps even eager, to bring Catholicism within the circle of toleration. He remains wary, however, since the noxious doctrines remain officially ensconced in Church doctrine. What has changed, it appears, is his estimate of the degree to which these were actively espoused by English Catholics in his day. If the noxious doctrines are effectively a dead letter for believers, Catholics can be as good citizens as others. We may say the same thing about Muslims, as Locke brings them into the argument of the *Letter* as a kind of parallel or stand-in for Catholicism. In cases like these, the critical issue for Locke (and for any who follow Locke's teaching on toleration) is practical, not theological. A religion that espouses practical doctrines subversive of civil law might still be eligible for toleration. This would depend, however, on a practical judgment that the doctrines in question are not actually being observed by the faithful, and there is no reasonable prospect that they will be. This process would be considerably eased, of course, by an official repudiation of those doctrines by the religious hierarchy itself.

If these conditions are met, many of the principles listed by Locke on the first page of the Annapolis Manuscript—"Reasons for tolerating Papists equally with others"—would come into play. These are general principles of toleration toward all religions: persecution alienates precisely the "best sort" among any persecuted sect; members of the sect in question are just as good citizens as members of any other sect; all subjects ought to be equally "countenanced and employed" by the prince, lest he lose the services of any of his subjects; ability alone should be the criterion of advancement in public careers; toleration endears all subjects to the prince who receive from him protection for their beliefs; and finally, coercion is "contrary to the rule of religion" and is ineffectual in any case. These are the principles that Locke has bequeathed to his posterity. Lockean toleration is capacious, but it does not tolerate practices or allegiances subversive of the political order. Churches must join the Lockean social contract, as it were, and purge themselves of any such practices in order to come within Lockean toleration. The evolution of Locke's own thought illuminates this for us today. Lockean toleration has prevailed for so long in the West that we scarcely remember—we scarcely need to remember—the limits to it. If more recent events have forced us to ponder those limitations again, Locke's account of the reasons for toleration, and the reasons for those limits, might help guide the cause of toleration today.

Transcript of the Annapolis Manuscript

[Marginal numbers refer to the relevant pages of the Wolseley pamphlet]

<manuscript p 1>
Reasons for tolerating Papists equally with others

7Persecution disobliges the best sort amongst the papists as well as amongst others.

12 If liberty of conscience make all men daily more & more to abhor popery papists may be tolerated as well as others.

13 If liberty of conscience breed men up in an irreconcilable dislike to all imposition in religion, papists may be safely tolerated.

If liberty of conscience unite the protestants against the papists, papists may safely be tolerated.

15 If toleration be the way to convert papists as well as others, they may equally be tolerated.

16 If papists can be supposed to be as good subjects as others they may be equally tolerated.

17 If all subjects should be equally countenanced & employed by the prince, the papists have an equal title.

If abilities alone ought to prefer men to employment & the king ought not to lose the use of any part of his subjects, papists are to be tolerated.

If liberty of conscience oblige all parties to the prince & make them wholly depend upon him, then the papists may be tolerated.

18 If to force dissenters to one's opinion be contrary to the rule of religion & to no purpose, papists should be tolerated.

20 If suffering for it will promote any opinion, papists are to be tolerated.

<manuscript p 2>

Pag. 3 The papists can be as little satisfied with or reconciled to the government by toleration as restraint. Liberty of conscience being here intended to unite the protestants in one common interest, under one protector in opposition to them & so cannot oblige them.

3 Persecution of them alone can as little make them unite with the other parties, as toleration can make them divide amongst themselves. Both which effects follow a general toleration or persecution of other dissenters.

4 In punishing papists for their religion, you are not so liable to mistake by prosecuting that as faction which is indeed conscience, as in persecuting other dissenters. For those who are absolutely disposed of by an authority supposed infallible, whose interest is directly opposite to yours, must necessarily be all factious however some of them may be sincerely conscientious.

5 Though persecution usually makes other opinions be sought after & admired; yet perhaps it is less apt to recommend popery then any other religion. 1st because persecution is its own practice & so begets less pity. 2^{ndly} The principles & doctrines of that religion seem less apt to take inquisitive heads or unstable minds, men commonly in their voluntary changes do rather pursue liberty & enthusiasm, wherein they seem their own disposers, rather then give themselves up to the authority & imposition of others. Besides if popery, having been brought in & continued by power & force joined with the art & industry of the clergy, it is the most likely of any religion <manuscript p 3> to decay, where the secular power handles them severely or at least takes from them those encouragements & supports they receive from their own clergy.

Query: Whether the papists or protestants gained most proselytes by the persecutions they suffered in those changes at the beginning of the reformation.

7 Standers-by will be less dissatisfied with severity used to papists than to others because it is lex talionis. Besides he cannot be thought to be punished merely for conscience who owns himself at the same time the subject and adherent of an enemy prince.

8 That a prince ought to encourage knowledge, from whence spring vanity of opinions in religion, makes not at all for papists who own an implicit faith & acquiesce in ignorance & who may as well submit to the impositions of their own lawful prince, as those of a foreigner, the infallibility of both sides being equal.

All the rest that is said p. 8 favours the toleration of papists less than others.

9 Twill be less dangerous to discontent the papists when the other parties are pleased than now. Especially when indulgence will less secure you of their fidelity to the government than that of others. Every subject has an interest in his naturall prince, whilst he does not own subjection to another power.

Liberty will less destroy the hopes & pretensions of papists that desire public mischief, than of others. Because they are backed by a foreign power & are obliged to propagate their religion by force.

A small part of the trade of England is (I think) managed by papists & if imposition in religion will lessen their trade <manuscript p 4> tis perhaps a reason why they should not be tolerated.

If it be the king's interest to be head of the protestants this bespeaks no indulgence for papists unless the persecuting of them here will draw the same usage or worse upon the protestants beyond sea. And how far even that may be advantageous to us in the present posture of affairs can only be determined by those who can judge whether the Huguenots in France or papists in England are likeliest to make head & disturb the respective governments.

11 I doubt whether upon protestant principles we can justify punishing of papists for their speculative opinions, as purgatory [or] transubstantiation if they stopped there. But possibly no reason nor religion obliges us to tolerate those whose practical principles necessarily lead them to the eager persecution of all opinions & the utter destruction of all societies but their own, so that it is not the difference of their opinion in religion, or of their ceremonies in worship, but their dangerous & factious tenets in reference to the state (which are blended with & make a part of their religion) that exclude them from the benefit of toleration. Who would think it fit to tolerate either Presbyterian or independent, if they made it a part of their religion to pay in implicit subjection to a foreign infallible power?

13 Severity to papists only, cannot make them unite with any other party nor toleration disunite them among themselves.

3.

LOCKE'S "APPEAL TO HEAVEN:" JEPHTHAH, CONSCIENCE, AND THE RIGHT OF RESISTANCE

Gabrielle Stanton Ray

Introduction

One of the central teachings of Locke's *Second Treatise* is his doctrine on the right of resistance. In short, this is the view that government is vested with its power through the consent of the people, which it is meant to exercise toward a specific end: the protection of their lives, liberties, and estates, all of which Locke captures under the heading of "property" (*2T* 123).[1] When the government acts to undermine this end, the people are entitled to reclaim their natural liberty, resist the present political authority, and form their own legislative anew (*2T* 240).

Locke often describes this decision to resist in terms of making an "Appeal to Heaven" (*2T* 20).[2] Broadly speaking, the phrase applies to any instance in which an individual, or group of individuals, find themselves party to a conflict wherein they are unable to appeal to the law as a means of resolution. Such a scenario arises either because (a) the parties of the conflict are in a state of nature (whether interpersonal or international) in which there exists *no common judge* to whom to appeal for relief, or (b) the conflict happens within civil society, where the otherwise legal avenues of relief are obstructed

---

[1] John Locke, *Two Treatises on Government,* ed. Peter Laslett (Cambridge: University Press, 1960). Hereafter, citations for the *Second Treatise* will be denoted by *2T* and section number, e.g. (*2T* 123).

[2] See also *2T* 21, 168, 176, 240–241.

through a perversion of justice (*2T* 20). In both cases, "War is made upon the sufferers, who having no appeal on Earth to right them, they are left to the only remedy in such Cases, an appeal to Heaven" (*2T* 20). When applied to case (b), to "Appeal to Heaven" therefore becomes synonymous with resistance or revolution.

But of *what* precisely, does an "Appeal to Heaven" actually consist for Locke, and in what sense does it provide a "remedy" for the situation? It is important to note that, for Locke, an "Appeal to Heaven" is *not* to expect God's literal intervention in the conflict, nor to ask God to reveal his judgment of the conflict by determining its outcome. On the contrary, Locke insists that while God is "judge," his judgment on human actions will not come until the end of days (*2T* 21). Thus, to "Appeal to Heaven" is not to ask something of *God*, but rather to make a statement to other *men;* it is to declare one's self-assurance in the rightness of one's cause, from the standpoint of that "Law antecedent and paramount to all positive Laws of men" (*2T* 168).

Put simply, to "Appeal to Heaven" is not only to take action, but also to have what I will call "confidence in conscience" in one's right to do so—and this is a confidence one can claim only after serious reflection. For the question at stake is not simply *how* to respond to someone else's having placed themselves into a state of war with me, but *whether* they have indeed done so. Moreover, this confidence includes a readiness to be held accountable for the potential practical consequences of that action. Locke captures both of these requirements—confidence in conscience, and readiness to be held accountable—in his solemn warning that someone who "Appeals to heaven,"

> must be sure he has Right on his side; and a Right too that is worth the Trouble and Cost of the Appeal, as he will answer at a Tribunal, that cannot be deceived, and will be sure to retribute to every one according to the Mischiefs he hath created to his Fellow-Subjects; that is, any part of Mankind. (*2T* 176)

As we can begin to see, Locke's stipulations for political resistance, when expressed in terms of making an "Appeal to Heaven," place a heavy moral burden on those considering resistance. Yet despite Locke's dire warnings to those considering such action, the *Second Treatise* has generally been taken to be a staunch defense of the right of resistance. However, in this chapter I would like to take a step back, and seriously consider the implications of Locke's teaching on resistance in terms of making an "Appeal to Heaven," and what that requires in terms of "confidence of conscience." When considered in the context of these requirements, several difficulties for our understanding of Locke's genuine view on the right of resistance arise.

To begin with, the heavy moral burden Locke places on the consciences of those considering resistance seems almost impossible to meet in light of the more skeptical comments Locke makes elsewhere in regard to the faculty of conscience, and man's capacity for moral knowledge in general. In some of his earlier writings, as well as in the *Essay Concerning Human Understanding,* Locke takes an almost Hobbesian attitude towards conscience, defining it more in terms of opinion than of moral certainty. And even in the *Second Treatise* itself Locke stresses the natural obstructions—namely, self-interest and the passions—that preclude our knowing and practicing the Law of Nature. Put simply, by trusting humans to make weighty decisions in accordance with "calm reason and conscience" (*2T* 8), Locke amplifies the human's capacity for moral reasoning in ways that seem to extend beyond what he elsewhere allows.[3]

These apparent theoretical inconsistencies are compounded upon consideration of a puzzling literary conceit contained in the *Second Treatise.* This is the problem—or rather the host of problems—introduced by the Old Testament figure Jephthah, whom Locke references a total of four times in the *Second Treatise* (plus

---

[3] Lee Ward makes a similar point, but specifically in regard to Locke's discussion of the natural right of punishment, which I will discuss briefly below. See Lee Ward, "Locke on Punishment, Property and Moral Knowledge," *Journal of Moral Philosophy*, 6 (2009): 218–244.

once in the *First*).[4] Apart from Adam, this makes Jephthah the most frequently cited Biblical character in the *Second Treatise*, and yet his importance for Locke is often overlooked.[5] In three out of those five references, Jephthah is mentioned as a model of someone making an "Appeal to Heaven." As such, Jephthah becomes something of a "poster boy" for the concept of appealing to a higher power; presumably, for the enduring authority of Natural Law even in circumstances which might otherwise be characterized by legal or normative anarchy.

In some ways, Jephthah, who appears in the eleventh chapter of Judges, is a fitting choice for this role. His Israelite tribe is engaged in a conflict over land rights with a neighboring tribe (the Ammonites), and while both sides put forth claims for the land, there is no common judge to adjudicate the dispute. After a failed attempt at international diplomacy, Jephthah gives up, announcing: "Let the Lord, who is judge, decide today for the Israelites or for the Ammonites" (Judges 11:27).[6] Thus, Jephthah's so-called "Appeal to Heaven."

But Locke's use of the Jephthah narrative proves problematic. First, Jephthah's "Appeal to Heaven" is an appeal to God to render divine judgment *today*, by interceding in the events of *this* world. Yet, as noted, Locke's "Appeal to Heaven" is a declaration before man of one's willingness to be judged in the *next* world.[7] Second,

---

[4] The *First Treatise* reference occurs at 163. The *Second Treatise* references are at 21, 109, 176, and 241.

[5] Notable exceptions are Andrew Rehfeld, "Jephthah, the Hebrew Bible, and John Locke's 'Second Treatise on Government,'" *Hebraic Political Studies*, vol. 3, no. 1 (Winter 2008): 60–93, and Samuel Moyn, "Appealing to Heaven: Jephthah, John Locke, and Just War," *Hebraic Political Studies*, vol. 4, no. 3 (Summer 2009): 286–303.

[6] Citations to *Judges* are from Robert Alter's Hebrew Bible translation. Robert Alter, *Ancient Israel: The Former Prophets: Joshua, Judges, Samuel, and Kings* (New York: W.W. Norton & Company, 2013), 105-183.

[7] Andrew Rehfeld also identifies this discrepancy in the immediacy of judgment. See Rehfeld, "Jephthah," 72.

the Biblical Jephthah story depicts a conflict *between* nations, ambiguous as regards to which nation is truly in the right. Yet, Locke uses the figure of Jephthah to defend the right of resistance against *one's own* (tyrannical) government. We are therefore left to wonder whether these two situations are appropriately analogous. Finally— and most damningly— Locke cites Jephthah as a sort of heroic spokesman for Natural Law. Yet, in doing so, Locke omits crucial parts of the story that reveal Jephthah as a true villain before Natural Law: On the eve of battle, directly following his "Appeal," Jephthah makes a second transaction with God. Jephthah vows that if God will bring victory over the Ammonites, he, Jephthah, will offer as a burnt sacrifice whoever is first to come out of his house to greet him upon his return. Returning home, the first person to greet him is his beloved daughter, his only child. Although it causes him great anguish, Jephthah goes through with the sacrifice.

This "vow" episode—concealed by Locke— is violently opposed to central Lockean principles. In both the *First* and *Second Treatise,* Locke repeatedly declares that parents have a natural duty to "preserve and cherish" their children. Locke writes that this duty is "a charge so incumbent on parents for their children's good, that nothing can absolve them from taking care of it" (*2T* 67). And, notably, "nothing" *includes* any vow or contract. A parent "cannot by any compacts whatsoever, bind his children or posterity" (*2T* 116). Accordingly, any vow made by a parent that would compromise the child's safety is null. Even in the *Essay,* where Locke denies the existence of innate principles, he acknowledges the overwhelming naturalness of the duty for parents to "preserve and cherish" their children (*ECHU* I.3.12).[8] The careful reader should therefore be perplexed as to why Locke uses Jephthah as a spokesman for "appealing to heaven," and all that entails regarding "confidence of conscience." Why does Locke choose, as a model for this concept, a

---

[8] John Locke, *An Essay Concerning Human Understanding,* ed. Peter H. Nidditch (Oxford: Oxford University Press, 1975). Hereafter cited as *ECHU,* by book, chapter, and section.

figure who is not so much a hero for Natural Law, as he is a villain?

While I do not promise to answer these questions in full, what I do hope to accomplish in the present chapter is to tease out some of the puzzles surrounding Locke's use of Jephthah, and demonstrate why Locke's use of Jephthah should give us pause when appraising Locke's views on "Appealing to Heaven" and the right of resistance. I will begin in §1 by providing an overview of Locke's resistance theory and the various frameworks in which he expresses it, and then consider some of the tensions that exist in that theory even independent of the Jephthah problem. In §2 I will take a closer look at the Jephthah narrative as a whole and the unique problems it introduces, and in §3 I will consider some of those problems in light of the rich history of commentary on the Jephthah story, in order to demonstrate that Locke and his readers would have been aware of the full story. Finally, I will provide a preliminary hypothesis as to the meaning of this strange puzzle.

§1. Locke's Resistance Theory

In this section, I will provide a brief overview of Locke's argument for the right of resistance within the three following, interrelated frameworks: (1) Locke's resistance theory as an upshot of his "social contract" argument (§1.1); (2) resistance theory as an extension of Locke's "strange doctrine" on the natural right of punishment in the state of nature (§1.2); and (3) Locke's resistance theory as characterized by the right of making an "Appeal to Heaven" (§1.3). Finally (§1.4), I will mention some of the tensions that exist within Locke's account of the right of resistance, independent of those introduced by Jephthah.

§1.1 The Right to Resistance as an Upshot of Social Contract Theory. Broadly speaking, Locke presents his argument regarding the right of resistance in the *Second Treatise* in the framework of what we commonly refer to as social contract theory. That is, Locke regards political power as an authority generated "by compact" (*2T* 171), thereby locating the basis of political authority in the rational, preservation-oriented consent of the people (*2T* 128, 163, 168).

Members of the society relinquish their natural liberty in exchange for protection of their "property"—that is, their lives, liberties and estates—which would be insecure in a state of unlimited natural freedom (*2T* 123). Therefore, any time the government makes any kind of "design" (*2T* 225) against the people's lives, liberties or properties, it can be seen as undermining the very "end" for which it was established, and the people are entitled to resist (*2T* 240). Notably, Locke characterizes this resistance in terms of self-defense, which is why he refrains from using the term "rebellion" to describe the action whereby the people retain their original supremacy. On the contrary, he emphasizes that the true "rebel" is the one who had initially placed himself into a state of war with the rest of the people (*2T* 226). Thus, in resisting a king or legislative that has abused the trust placed in it by the people, the latter are merely taking back into their own hands that which they had originally, collectively resigned up to the government for the sake of the protection of their property—their natural right to self-preservation. It is important to note, however, that this natural right to self-preservation is only one half of the dual "political power" (*2T* 128, 171) that men have by nature. The other half of this dual power is a bit more surprising, but just as important to Locke's argument: it is the natural right of punishment. Indeed, as we shall see, political resistance can be understood as an extension, or perhaps a "reactivation," of both the natural power of preservation and the natural power of punishment, to which we now turn.

§1.2. Resistance as an Expression of the Natural Right of Punishment. Locke admits that his teaching on the natural right of punishment is a "very strange Doctrine" (*2T* 9), although he does not fully explain exactly what makes it so strange.[9] Perhaps it is strange because of the moral nature of punishment, and we are accustomed to imagining— *á la* Hobbes—the state of nature as a condition in which

---

[9] For a discussion of this puzzle, see Lee Ward, "Locke on Punishment," 222–228.

nothing can be just or unjust.[10] By contrast, Locke's state of nature (at least at first glance), is governed in a much more robust way by the Law of Nature; it commands, in addition to self-preservation, a positive duty to preserve the rest of mankind (2T 6). It is therefore possible, in Locke's state of nature, for one individual to commit a "crime" against the Law of Nature by infringing against the life, liberty, or property of another. Such a criminal is then deserving of punishment—either by the victims of their crime, or any other third party acting on the victim's behalf (2T 11). In committing a crime even against just one person, the criminal has placed himself into a "State of War" with the entire human species (2T 11). Therefore, any member of the entire species has a right, by nature, to punish the criminal, as an act of self-defense and a warning to others.

To be in a state of war is essentially to be engaged in a conflict (or, in this case, to have been the victim of a crime), in which there is no common judge to whom to appeal for relief or to adjudicate the dispute (2T 19). Consider the distinction Locke makes between a "state of war" and a "state of nature" (properly speaking) in Chapter II of the *Second Treatise:* "Men living together according to reason, without a common Superior on Earth, with Authority to judge between is *properly the State of Nature*" (2T 19). By supposed contrast: "force, or a declared design of force, upon the Person of another, where there is no common Superior on Earth *to appeal to for relief, is the State of War*" (2T 19). While both conditions are marked by the absence of a common judge, what separates a state of war from a state of nature is simply that this absence makes itself felt when a crime has been committed and there is no avenue for relief.

This way of distinguishing between a state of nature and a state of war also allows Locke to describe several other scenarios *outside* the state of nature as "states of war." Within civil society, it can exist (a) in momentary instances, when a crime is committed and the victim doesn't have time to wait on the law for relief, or (b) when the rights of the people broadly speaking are violated, and though ave-

---

[10] Thomas Hobbes, *Leviathan*, ed. Edwin Curley (Indianapolis: Hackett, 1994), 78.

nues for legal relief do lie open, they are obstructed by the government itself (*2T* 20). Finally, a state of war can exist (c) internationally, when there is no common judge to adjudicate disputes *between* distinct societies.[11] Through the second option, Locke forges an analogy between criminals in the state of nature and rulers within society who abuse their trust—thereby, between the natural right of punishment and the right of resistance.

Locke makes this analogy even more memorable through the colorful language he uses to describe both criminals in the state of nature, and, as we later find, tyrants within civil society.

In both cases, Locke describes the perpetrators as wild animals—as "lyons," "tygers" and sometimes "wolves"[12]— strongly suggesting that not only do they pose a lethal threat to other humans, but also that, through their crime, they somehow demote themselves from the status of those sharing the defining attribute of Reason. He describes a criminal in the state of nature as one who has "renounced Reason...declared War against all Mankind, and therefore may be destroyed as a *Lyon* or a *Tyger*" (*2T* 11). He uses similar language of universal ostracization when describing a tyrant: he is "guilty of the greatest Crime, I think, a Man is capable of...the common Enemy and Pest of Mankind; and is to be treated accordingly" (*2T* 230).

On both of these levels—the natural right of punishment and its "expression" in the right of resistance—Locke stresses that the power to punish is *not* an arbitrary power, by which he means it is not the power "to use a Criminal when he has got him in his hands, according to the passionate heats, or boundless extravagancies of his own Will" (*2T* 8). Rather, it is the power "only to retribute to him, so far as *calm reason and conscience dictates,* what is proportionate to his Transgression" (*2T* 8). Let us keep the "calm reason and conscience" requirement in mind, as it will come up again when we consider the natural right of punishment in its alternative manifesta-

---

[11] Locke will not mention this option until his chapter on Conquest, but it is implied by the Jephthah narrative (*2T* 21).

[12] See also *2T* 7, 10, 16, 17, 93, 172, and 230.

tion—"Appealing to Heaven."

§1.3. Resistance as making an "Appeal to Heaven:" Jephthah and the Role of Conscience. In addition to "punishment," Locke uses the language of "Appealing to Heaven" to describe the appropriate response to a situation of judicial anarchy; i.e., when a violation has been perpetrated, but there is no judge to whom to appeal for relief. Thus—and even more strongly than is the case with punishment— "Appealing to Heaven" becomes a stand-in term for political resistance: in both cases, *"War is made* upon the Sufferers, who having no appeal on Earth to right them, they are left to the only remedy in such Cases, an appeal to Heaven" (*2T* 20).

Presumably, Locke uses the character of Jephthah to illustrate both the condition of judicial anarchy and the action made in response to it. Jephthah is engaged in a conflict with the Ammonites in which both sides put forth claims regarding their respective rights to the land in question, but there is no judge to weigh these claims. As Locke retells the story:

> Had there been any such Court, any superior Jurisdiction on Earth, to determine the right between *Jephthah* and the *Ammonites,* they had never come to a State of War, but we see he was forced to appeal to *Heaven. The Lord the Judge* (says he) *be Judge this day between the Children of* Israel *and the Children of* Ammon, *Judg.* 11.27. and then Prosecuting, and relying on his *appeal,* he leads out his Army to Battle. (*2T* 21, emphasis in original)

To begin with, we can see that, on the most direct and concrete level, the phrase "Appeal to Heaven" does not entail *God's* intervention in human affairs—whether immediate, or delayed— but rather the actual, *human action* taken in the here and now, in response to having been placed in a state of war (in Jephthah's case, leading his army into battle; in the cases of victims of tyranny, resistance in whatever that entails).

But if to "Appeal to Heaven" is simply a euphemism for human action in this life, why describe it in terms of heaven at all? There is a deeper and more psychological component to appealing to heaven too, which does involve a delay in judgment, and which we can get at when we consider the following questions: What does Locke's Jephthah mean when he calls upon the Lord to be "Judge" of the conflict? And what does Locke mean when he says that Jephthah proceeds to "rely on his appeal" as he leads out his army into battle? Locke's following statement provides a somewhat obscure answer:

> And therefore in such Controversies, where the question is put, *who shall be Judge?* It cannot be meant, who shall decide the Controversy; every one knows what *Jephtha* here tells us, that *the Lord the Judge* shall judge. Where there is no Judge on Earth, the *Appeal* lies to God in Heaven. That Question then cannot mean, who shall judge? whether another hath put himself in a State of War with me, and whether I may as *Jephtha* did, appeal to Heaven in it? Of that I myself can only be Judge in my own Conscience, as I will answer it at the great Day, to the Supream Judge of all Men. (*2T* 21)[13]

It is not entirely clear from this passage in just what sense God will "be Judge." According to Locke's analysis (and despite his account of the Biblical story, in which Jephthah calls upon God to be judge "*this day*"), God will be the judge of the controversy only at "the great Day." This means that humans must choose their actions *today*, knowing that someday God will judge them, and yet *not* knowing for sure what God's judgment will be. In the meantime,

---

[13] Locke's answer here is admittedly awkward, and difficult to decipher. Fortunately he provides a somewhat clearer answer in a later passage, where he poses in almost identical terms the question of "Who shall be Judge?" when it comes to a dispute in which there is no earthly adjudicator: "This Question, (*Who shall be Judge?*) cannot mean, that there is no Judge at all. For where there is no Judicature on Earth, to decide Controversies amongst Men, *God* in Heaven is *Judge:* He alone, 'tis true, is Judge of the Right. But *every Man* is *Judge* for himself, as in all other Cases, so in this, whether another hath put himself into a State of War with him, and whether he should appeal to the Supreme Judge, as *Jephtha* did" (*2T* 241).

they themselves must make a "judgment" of what God's verdict will be. Thus, what Locke wants to stress here is not so much what God will be judge of at the end of days, as what each *individual* must be judge of now—in his "own Conscience."[14] More specifically, as we can see from the quote above, the content of the judgment at stake is *whether* one's opponent has indeed placed themselves into a state of war first, and whether one is therefore morally permitted to strike. And this judgment takes place in a separate, prior examination of Conscience, which is only a lead-up to the moment in which the *action* of the "Appeal" occurs. The major takeaway is that to "Appeal to Heaven" implies that the individual making the appeal acknowledges that, one day (that "great Day"), God will judge everyone, and the one appealing will be ready to be held accountable for his choice and its consequences. In other words, to make an "Appeal to Heaven" is similar to making an oath, in the strict sense of the term. It is essentially to say, with confidence: *I believe in my conscience that this is the right course of action, and so help me God if I am wrong.*

Locke states this "confidence in conscience" requirement a bit more strongly later in the *Second Treatise,* where he is discussing the rights of unjustly conquered people and their descendants. After claiming that the latter have the right to appeal for a rectification of injustice on behalf of their ancestors, Locke claims "they may *appeal,* as *Jephtha* did, to *Heaven,* and repeat their *Appeal* till they have recovered the native Right of their Ancestors" (*2T* 176). But then, Locke adds a more moderating set of qualifications: he who appeals must be sure that (1) he has right on his side, and (2) that even if he *is* in the right, he is confident that his is a cause worth the (potentially grave) costs of pursuing it—and worth it not only from his standpoint, but from *any part of mankind* (*2T* 176—see quote in Introduction). On top of these requirements, Locke identifies cer-

---

[14] As Andrew Rehfeld puts it, "Locke's reference to 'God as judge' is meant only to clarify the stakes involved in such an appeal and to conceptually establish a judge before whom such claims are made." Rehfeld, "Jephthah," 70.

tain practical limitations on "Appealing to Heaven." For example, after claiming that the people retain the right to "Appeal to heaven" when judging the "Old Question" of whether their prince has made a right use of his prerogative, Locke insists that this right "operates not till the Inconvenience is so great, that the Majority feel it, and are weary of it, and find a necessity to have it amended" (*2T* 168).

Locke places similar breaks on his right to resistance in passages where he talks about it more directly, and not just through the euphemism of "Appealing to Heaven." For example, in Chapter XVIII, "Of Tyranny," Locke presents a series of reasons why his doctrine on the right to resist a tyrant won't easily lead to "Danger or Confusion" (*2T* 204). First, he says, in some countries the prince is viewed as sacred, which means he is immune to criticism and violence. Instead, his subordinates will likely become the scapegoats for the people's complaints, and Locke says it is "safer" for a few private men to suffer than for the "head of the Republick [to be] easily, and upon slight occasions exposed" (*2T* 205). In countries where the king is *not* viewed as sacred, the doctrine still won't lead to rebellion so long as avenues for legal relief exist (*2T* 207). But what about when the princely authority *obstructs* those avenues?[15] Even then, Locke claims "the *Right of resisting...will not* suddenly, or on slight occasions, *disturb the Government*" (*2T* 208). Again, in order for discontent with the government to reach the point of resistance, it would have to be extremely widespread—"it being impossible for one or a few oppressed Men to *disturb the Government*, where the Body of the People do not think themselves concerned in it" (*2T* 208). On the contrary, it will take a "long train of Abuses, Prevarications and Artifices" for the people at large to take notice (*2T* 225).[16] At which point, Locke concedes, if the people are "perswaded in their Consciences that their Laws and with them their Estates, liberties, and Lives are in danger, and perhaps their

---

[15] Recall that this is one key variation of a "state of war" that Locke mentions in *2T* 21.

[16] Notice the similarity in language to the American Declaration of Independence.

Religion too, how they will be hindered from resisting illegal force, used against them, I cannot tell" (*2T* 209). At this point, the government is in "the most dangerous state" it can possibly be in. *But,* he assures the reader, it is also "so easie to be avoided" (*2T* 209). The reason it is "so easie"? As long as the King governs his people as a father does his children, he will remain in favor with them: "It being impossible for a Governour, if he really means the good of his People…not to make them see and feel it; as it is for the Father of a Family, not to let his Children see he loves, and takes care of them" (*2T* 209).

§1.4 Preliminary Problems with Locke's Resistance Theory. In the following section, we will take a closer look at the Jephthah story in order to see the problems it introduces for the "Appeal to Heaven" and, thereby, for Locke's resistance theory in general. But before Jephthah even enters the picture, there are already some tensions lurking in Locke's resistance theory as I have outlined it above, which we shall consider briefly now.

First, recall that for Locke the right to resistance is rooted in the natural right of punishment. In punishment (and also in resistance) Locke expects those taking action to do so in accordance with "calm reason and conscience." But this expectation is entirely inconsistent with his later concessions regarding the "inconveniencies" (*2T* 127) of the state of nature, which he lists most concisely in Chapter IX. The first deficiency is the lack of an "*establish'd, settled, known Law*" to serve as the "common measure" to decide controversies. Although the Law of Nature "be plain and intelligible to all rational Creatures," men are either "ignorant for want of any study of it," or biased by their own self-interest from applying it objectively (*2T* 124). The second deficiency is the lack of a "*known and indifferent judge*" with authority to decide controversies. In the state of nature, each individual serves as his own judge of the Law of Nature, but this is problematic because, again, men will be partial to themselves. In addition, 'Passion and Revenge is very apt to carry them too far, and with too much heat, in their own Cases; as well as negligence, and unconcernedness, to make them too remiss, in all other Mens" (*2T* 125). Finally, the third deficiency is that "there often wants *Power* to back and support the Sentence when right, and to *give* it due *Execution*" (*2T* 126). Locke's reasoning here is more practical in nature: because those who committed the crimes in the first place are prone to force and violence, it will be difficult and dangerous to attempt to punish them.

What we see here is a far cry from the image of the state of nature Locke initially gives us in Chapter II— in which those who violate the Laws of Nature are implied to be outliers, villains, and beasts who demote themselves from the rest of the (presumably rational) species of human beings. Now it turns out that to stray from the Laws of Nature is not so much the exception as it is the rule. In general, men are "biased" in favor of their particular self-interest, prone to irrational passions in their own cases, and just plain indifferent when it comes to the trials of others. So much for justice on behalf of the underdog in the state of nature.

Similar problems haunt Locke's account of resistance in terms of appealing to Heaven, and the confidence in conscience that entails. Recall that in appealing to heaven, I must have confidence in conscience that (1) right is on my side and, (2) the end of my "appeal" is *worth* whatever costs I will incur in making it. Setting aside the practical impossibility of meeting the second requirement, does Locke really believe that when people decide to "Appeal to Heaven," they do so only after careful reflection, in which they make sure their motives are in accord with objective moral principles? If we are to give any weight to Locke's earlier writings, he certainly does not. In his *Two Tracts on Government*, for example—where Locke disparagingly defines conscience as "nothing but an opinion of the truth of any practical position" (*First Tract* 138)[17]—Locke expresses great concern over people's tendency to *abuse* so-called "conscience claims," especially with regard to things they claim are necessary for their salvation. There is nothing so indifferent for salvation, Locke

---

[17] John Locke, "First Tract on Government," in *Two Tracts on Government*, ed. Philip Abrams (Cambridge: Cambridge University Press, 1967).

warns, that someone, somewhere won't make a fuss about it on the grounds of "conscience" (*First Tract* 138).

Moreover, the fact that men are generally "biased in their own interest, or misled by their ignorance and indiscretion" means that they are "ill judges of reasons of state or the equity of laws" (*First Tract* 137–138). And Locke makes dire warnings about the epistemic anarchy that can result when people are given free rein to consult their "consciences" when deciding whether to obey the law: "Nor can a subject's vow or private error of conscience nullify the edicts of the magistrate, for if this is once granted, discipline will be everywhere at an end...each would be his own Lawmaker and his own God" (*Second Tract* 226–227).[18] He also warns that it is not long before this epistemic anarchy leads to actual danger: "Do but once arm their consciences against the magistrate and their hands will not long be idle or innocent" (*First Tract* 154). Indeed, Locke goes to far as to suggest that "conscience claims" were largely to blame for the chaos in recent English history (i.e. the English Civil War and its aftermath): "a liberty for tender consciences was the first inlet to all those confusions and unheard of and destructive opinions that threatened this nation" (*First Tract* 160). He also expresses great concern about the ability of the educated few to win the masses to their cause by wielding "the banners of liberty and conscience, those two watchwords of wonderful effect in winning support" (*Second Tract* 211).

By the time Locke writes the *Essay Concerning Human Understanding*—which he composes concomitantly with the *Second Treatise*—his rhetoric in his discussions about conscience (though sparse) is significantly toned down. However, there he more explicitly dismisses the view of Conscience as some kind of internal faculty that keeps our motives calibrated with the Law of Nature (*ECHU* I.3.7). On the contrary, he claims the origin of so-called Conscience in opinion, which can have a variety of sources: "*Perswasion, however*

---

[18] John Locke, "Second Tract on Government," in *Two Tracts on Government*, ed. Philip Abrams (Cambridge: Cambridge University Press, 1967).

got, will serve to set Conscience to work, which is nothing else, but our own Opinion or Judgment of the Moral Rectitude or Pravity of our own Actions" (*ECHU* 1.3.8). "Persuasion, however got" means that even doctrines that may have begun as "superstitions" eventually "grow up into the dignity of principles in religion and morality" (*ECHU* I.3.22). To bring the picture full circle, these types of principles could very well be the grounds for conscientious "Appeals to Heaven."

This more skeptical view of conscience makes Locke's reassurances against "danger or confusion" in the *Second Treatise* a little less reassuring. For example, the reassurance Locke most often cites is that oppression needs to be widespread in order for the people to be stirred out of their complacency. But this dismissal disregards the role of so-called "teachers," and their ability to manipulate the masses into sedition under the banner of "conscience," which Locke expresses so much caution over in his earlier writings (see for example *First Tract* 121; *Second Tract* 211). The additional safeguards Locke lists against "perpetual disorder" are unsatisfying for other reasons.[19] For example, Locke's "easie" recipe for avoiding danger and confusion—for a king to govern his people as a father does his children—is ironic in light of his constant effort to refute Filmer's conflation of parental and political power. We see a similar inconsistency in Locke's claim that the King being viewed as sacred protects against disorder, which is alarming given Locke's crusade against the divine right theory of political power. What is going on beneath these disparities? Is Locke perhaps admitting a tension between liberty and stability?

Either way, there is a sense in which we can say that, considered thus far, Locke's resistance theory appears simultaneously radi-

---

[19]There are additional reasons that are empirical in nature. For example, Locke's claim that the network of scapegoats surrounding the king will protect the integrity of the commonwealth is clearly unsupported by relevant empirical evidence. Consider, for instance, the public campaigns against the Earl of Strafford and Archbishop Laud during the lead-up to the English Civil War, which only served to incite national tensions and were indeed precursors to the execution of the king himself.

cal and conservative. It is radical in theory, that is, insofar as his designation of the protection of "property" as the end of government creates a relatively low threshold for what constitutes a breach of contract on the part of the government. On the other hand, the requirements Locke places on someone considering resistance suggest that Locke is more cautious about resistance, and stingier with regard to the conditions he stipulates under which it is practically advisable or morally permissible. In fact, the moral burden Locke places on someone considering making an "Appeal to Heaven"—confidence in conscience of the righteousness of one's cause, and also that the end is worth the costs—is so heavy that one might wonder whether any act of resistance would pass Locke's test. Locke's exemplary "Appealer" should be one who is not only highly conscientious, but also possesses an almost superhuman ability to foresee future outcomes. If this is the case, then the model Locke *does* choose to illustrate the Appeal to Heaven—Jephthah—is highly inappropriate on both counts. As we shall see, not only is Jephthah blameworthy for the rashness with which he acts, but his gross miscalculation of future events brings about an outcome in which—in the words of Robert Herrick—"the cure was worse than the disease."[20]

§2. Jephthah: A Closer Look

In his five references to Jephthah throughout both *Treatises*,[21] Locke only mentions the first part of the narrative, the part of the story culminating in Jephthah's "Appeal to Heaven." Locke ignores what happens after the "Appeal," where Jephthah makes a second transaction with God in the form of "the Vow," ultimately resulting in his sacrifice of his own daughter. The second part of the narrative is most challenging to square with Locke, but as we shall see, there are problems in the first part as well. Let us begin by considering the

---

[20] Robert Herrick, "The Dirge for Jephthah's Daughter," in *The Hespirades & Noble Numbers*, ed. by Alfred Pollard (London/New York: Lawrence & Bullen, 1898).
[21] See footnote 4 above.

narrative as a whole.

§2.1. Jephthah: The Biblical Narrative. The Jephthah story occurs in the Book of Judges, the seventh book of the Old Testament.[22] Judges as a whole is a repetitive, vicious cycle in which the Israelites offend God, God punishes them, then takes pity on them; they offend again, and so on. Just before Jephthah enters the narrative (Judges 10), the Israelites are located in Gilead, where they have been dominated by a neighboring nation, the Ammonites, for 18 years. (An important fact, which will soon come into play, is that Gilead is actually land that the Israelites had originally conquered from a third tribe, the Amorites, over 300 years earlier). Now, the Ammonites are camped just outside of Gilead, which they plan on conquering with ease. The elders of Gilead gather together and agree that they must at least stand up against the Ammonites, agreeing that whoever leads them into battle will be their chief. The stage is set for Jephthah's entrance.

At this point, Jephthah is an outsider. The son of Gilead (and an implied prostitute), he had been initially banished from the tribe by his legitimate half-brothers (with the support of Gileadite elders) to ensure he did not try to claim their inheritance. Since his banishment, Jephthah has been "out riding" with a gang in the badlands, incurring a reputation for being a "valiant warrior." In

---

[22] For some commentators, it is not so much Jephthah as an individual as it is his place in Judges that is of significance for Locke. Peter Laslett, for example, says that Locke was likely influenced by the Calvinist view that "the Judges, Jephthah among them, represented a stage between the anarchy of primeval innocence and established sovereignty, a stage which inevitably passed because of the effects of the Fall." (See Laslett's footnote 17 to his edition of the *Two Treatises,* 282). John Thompson makes the interesting remark that the Jephthah story comes halfway through the book of Judges, a book which closes with the refrain: "in those days there was no King of Israel, the people did what was right in their own eyes." See Thompson, *Writing the Wrongs: Women of the Old Testament among Biblical Commentators from Philo through the Reformation* (Oxford: University Press, 2001), 100.

desperation, the Gileadite elders approach Jephthah and implore him to lead them into battle against the Ammonites; in return, they will make him chief (Judges 11: 1–11). After accepting the commission, Jephthah first attempts to extract a peaceful concession from the Ammonites. He sends a messenger to the Ammonite king, asking why the Ammonites seek to do battle against the Gileadites. The Ammonite king's answer is reasonable: the Gileadites are occupying land that they themselves had unlawfully conquered (Judges 11:12–13). But Jephthah rejects these arguments, objecting that (a) the Israelites had taken the land in question from the *Amorites*, not the Ammonites, and (b) they did so without injustice, as an act of self-defense (Judges 11:15–24). Moreover, if the Ammonites really thought that they had a rightful claim to the land, why did they wait 300 years to pursue it? (Judges 11:25–27). What is interesting about this exchange is that each side appeals to what it expects to be shared principles. This attempt to argue from "common ground" is most directly evident in Jephthah's argument that the Israelites' God had deliberately dispossessed the Amorites of the land in order to give it to the Israelites: "Do you not take possession of what Chemosh your god gives you to possess? And all that the LORD our God has given us to possess, of that we shall take possession" (Judges 11:24–25). In other words, Jephthah is asking the Ammonites to "put yourselves in our shoes": if the *Ammonites'* god had given them repossessed land, they would feel entitled to keep it too.[23]

None of these arguments having worked to persuade the Ammonites to relinquish their claim, Jephthah's messenger finally delivers what Locke calls Jephthah's "Appeal to Heaven":

---

[23] In his annotation to this section, Robert Alter notes that from the point of view of the Israelites living during this time period, it would not have been so strange for Jephthah's messenger to appeal to the existence of a rival god in making his argument: "The theological assumption of this statement is perfectly characteristic of this early period of Israelite history. Israel has its own God, YHWH ('the Lord'), believed to be more powerful than other gods, but each nation has its guiding deity, assumed to look after the national destiny." See Alter, *Ancient Israel*, 168, n. 24.

I on my part have committed no offense against you, yet you are doing evil to battle with me. Let the LORD, who is judge, judge today between the Israelites and the [Ammonites]. (Judges 11:27–28)

Thus, Jephthah prepares to lead his troops into battle. As the Biblical narrative tells us, "the spirit of the LORD was upon Jephthah, and he passed....on to the Ammonites" (Judges 11:29). However, it is important to note that at no point in the narrative does God actually "speak" or reveal his will. This is most conspicuously the case in the impending "Vow" episode, which the narrative reports Jephthah delivering directly after he passes on towards the Ammonites:

If You indeed give the Ammonites into my hand, it shall be that whatever comes out of the door of my house to meet me when I return safe and sound from the Ammonites shall be the LORD's, and I shall offer it up as a burnt offering. (Judges 11:30–32)[24]

Again, God is completely silent and neither sanctions nor condemns Jephthah's vow. As St. Augustine stresses in his analysis, even the narrator refrains from commentary; the text "neither praises nor condemns this oath, leaving us to exercise our intellect on the matter."[25] Still, Jephthah treats his vow as though it has generated a divine obligation from which he cannot receive exemption. After achieving victory—the narrative tells us that "the LORD gave [the Ammonites] into his hand"—Jephthah returns home, where the first person he encounters is his young daughter, who greets him

---

[24] Alter notes that what is translated as "whatever" is ambiguous in Hebrew; it could mean "whomever" (to refer specifically to a human being), or "whatever" to include animals as well. See Alter, *Ancient Israel,* 169, n.31.

[25] Augustine, *"Questiones in Heptateuchum,"* in *Patralogia Latina*, vol. xxxiv, ed. by J.P. Migne, 549–824 (Paris: Garnier: 1844–1879). As cited in Bernard Robinson, "The Story of Jephthah and his Daughter: Then and Now," *Biblica* vol. 85, no. 3 (2004): 334.

with "timbrels and dances" (Judges 11:33–35).

Jephthah's encounter with his daughter causes him great anguish; he tears at his own garments and laments "Alas, my daughter, you have indeed laid me low and you have joined ranks with my troublers, for I myself have opened my mouth to the LORD, and I cannot turn back" (Judges 11:35). While the precise content of the vow is never repeated, it is assumed that his daughter knows of her fate, as, with shocking complicity, she urges her father to "Do to me as it came out from your mouth." All she asks is for two months to lament her virginity in the wilderness beforehand, and Jephthah grants her request (Judges 11:36–38). When she returns after two months—still a virgin, the narrator confirms—Jephthah goes through with the sacrifice.[26] As the chapter closes, we are told that every year thereafter, the women of Israel would perform a traditional lament in memory of Jephthah's daughter (Judges 11:39–40).

§2.2 Problems for Locke, Independent of the "Vow." One way to dismiss the problems introduced by Jephthah's "Vow" is to propose that since Locke only mentions the "Appeal" part of the story, that's the only part relevant for his purposes. In §3 below, I will discuss why I do not think it is possible to separate the "Vow" from the "Appeal." But even if it were, the first part of the narrative (up to and including the Appeal) presents its own independent problems. For now, I will briefly touch on some of them.[27]

As Andrew Rehfeld notes, right off the bat the Jephthah narrative includes a violation of one of Locke's key principles when the Gileadite elders offer Jephthah the position of "chief" in exchange for his military leadership. For Locke, the legislative power of a state cannot delegate authority to a third party without the consent of the

---

[26] All we are told is that "he did to her as he had vowed," there are no other specifics given.

[27] Andrew Rehfeld has provided the most systematic exposition of these problems, and I recommend his excellent article for a more thorough treatment of them (Rehfeld, "Jephthah," 67–79).

people.[28] Another area where the Jephthah story seems at odds with Lockean principles has to do with the issue of conquest. It is not clear that, from a *Lockean* point of view, the Gileadites actually do have right on their side in their conflict with the Ammonites. According to Leo Strauss, they do not: in his brief discussion of Locke's use of Jephthah, Strauss notes that Locke "fails even to allude...to Jephthah's entirely un-Lockean view of the rights of the conqueror."[29] Recall, moreover, Jephthah's objection against the Ammonites' right to the land on the grounds that they waited 300 years to make their claim. But in Locke's discussion of conquest, the descendants of unjustly conquered people retain the right to "repeat their appeal" on behalf of their ancestors for generations to come.[30]

Then, there are problems with the "Appeal" itself. As I mentioned above, the Biblical account of Jephthah's appeal has him calling upon God to be judge of the conflict "today." Yet in his own analysis of what it means for "God to be judge," Locke repeatedly stresses that God is judge only at the *end* of days; to "rely" on one's appeal to God is more to make a promissory note in one's own conscience that one will be ready for judgment when the time comes.[31]

---

[28] Even if the Gileadite people are satisfied with the elders' choice, for Locke, retroactive "authorization" is not the same as and not a replacement for the initial consent whereby power is conferred. See Rehfeld, "Jephthah," 67–70.

[29] Leo Strauss, *Natural Right and History* (Chicago: University of Chicago Press, 1950), 214.

[30] As Rehfeld puts it, Jephthah seems to assume a "statute of limitations" for reclaiming land that Locke explicitly denies. Rehfeld, "Jephthah," 74.

[31] Rehfeld also stresses the inappropriateness of Locke's use of Jephthah in this regard: "Using Jephthah to illustrate an unanswered appeal to heaven is simply the most bizarre problem of biblical citation in the 'Second Treatise.'" (Rehfeld, "Jephthah," 72). Arthur Bradley adds that Locke's reading of the Jephthah narrative also undermines his own theory on religious toleration—specifically the separation of church and state—by featuring "a sovereign who resorts to his religious beliefs to solve a political dispute." Arthur Bradley, "Let the Lord the Judge be Judge: Hobbes and

Finally, Locke uses Jephthah's appeal to heaven—made in response to an *international* conflict—as the paradigm for appealing to heaven in response to a domestic conflict, but this is an imperfect analogy. For example, the "state of war" between the Gileadites and the Ammonites is not initiated by a breach of contract by one party against the other, as would be the case in Locke's account of a domestic "state of war" perpetrated by a tyrant against his people.

§2.3 The Filicide Problem. However, by far the most problematic aspect of the Jephthah narrative as a whole is what happens in the part of the story Locke excludes: the filicide. That Jephthah ends up going through with the sacrifice of his daughter has shocked readers for generations, but it is particularly problematic from a Lockean point of view. For Locke, the topic of parental power (and, just as importantly, its *limits*) plays a key role in both his political philosophy and his epistemology. In the *Essay Concerning Human Understanding*, Locke's primary project is to dismantle the notion of "Innate Ideas," both practical and speculative. While he therefore denies the innateness of any idea, he admits that "if any [idea] can be thought to be naturally imprinted, none, I think, can have a fairer pretense to be innate, than this: *parents preserve and cherish your children*" (*ECHU* I.3.12). What makes this principle feel so natural? Locke answers by distinguishing between "impressions of truth on the understanding" (which he denies) and "inclinations of the appetite to good" (which he allows):

> Nature, I confess, has put into man a desire of happiness, and an aversion to misery: these indeed are innate practical principles, which (as practical principles ought) do continue constantly to operate and influence all our actions...these may be observed in all persons and all ages, steady and universal. (*ECHU* I.3.3)

Locke on Jephthah, Liberalism and Martyrdom," *Law, Culture and the Humanities* (2017): 15.

One of these natural tendencies—perhaps the most intense—is of course the feeling of protection and affection parents have for their children. Locke develops this concept in both *Treatises*. In the *First Treatise*, he takes aim at Filmer's thesis on the father's absolute power over children. In response to Filmer's attempt to support this claim by citing the practice of child exposure, Locke wields language resonant of his discussion of criminals in the state of nature, denouncing exposure as a crime so grave it demotes its perpetrator *below* the status of animals. Exposure is

> the most shameful Action, and most unnatural Murder, humane nature is capable of. The Dens of Lions and Nurseries of Wolves know no such Cruelty as this: These Savage Inhabitants of the Desert obey God and Nature in being tender and careful of their Off-spring: They will Hunt, Watch, Fight, and almost Starve for the Preservation of their Young, never part with them, never forsake them till they are able to shift for themselves. (*1T* 56)

Similarly, in the *Second Treatise*, Locke insists that, to the extent parents do have authority over their children, this does not extend to a power of life and death (as Filmer claims), because parental power is "inseparably annexed" to the duty of parents to educate and nourish their children—a parent forfeits the former as soon as he abandons the latter (*2T* 65).[32] "God hath made it [parents'] business to imploy this Care on their Off-spring, and hath placed in them suitable Inclinations of Tenderness and Concern to Temper this power" (*2T* 63).[33]

---

[32] For Locke's arguments against parents' absolute, arbitrary power over their children—including the power of life and death as well as the power to dispense with their children's property—see also: *1T* 52–55, *2T* 56, 64, 171. In several of these cases Locke makes this argument on the basis of his "God's Workmanship" thesis.

[33] See *2T* 67, where Locke makes a similar point, claiming that, to the extent that parents are inclined towards "excess," it is more likely to lean on the side of leniency as opposed to severity. As an example meant to

Put simply, from Locke's point of view there is no justification for Jephthah's sacrifice of his daughter. What if Jephthah were to insist that his duty to perform his vow, as it was made to God, outweighs his parental duty? (In George Buchanan's retelling of the story, which we will discuss briefly below, this is in fact what Jephthah argues). But Locke would have none of this. Locke firmly insists that parents' "natural tenderness" is evidence of God's will that parental authority be exercised only toward the preservation, nourishment and education of the child (*1T* 56). Surely Locke would deny that God would require from Jephthah an act that goes against God's own will as expressed through nature. Furthermore, Locke would deny that Jephthah was authorized to bind his daughter to *anything* by virtue of his own contract: parents cannot make promises on behalf of their children. "'Tis true, that whatever Engagements or Promises any one has made for himself, he is under the Obligation of them, but *cannot* by any *Compact* whatsoever, bind *his Children* or Posterity" (*2T* 116). Similarly, he stresses that children should not be held accountable for the sins of their fathers (*2T* 180–182). In the biblical narrative, Jephthah uses language of blame against his daughter when he encounters her upon his return. He therefore treats his perceived obligation to sacrifice her as though it is caused by *her* actions instead of his own. This is of course unreasonable, especially from Locke's perspective.

Moreover, the fact that Jephthah's daughter is complicit in the sacrifice means nothing from Locke's point of view. For Locke, parents have a duty to preserve, nourish and educate their children in large part because children lack the understanding to direct their own wills (*2T* 58). Jephthah's daughter, as a child, cannot be understood as actually "consenting" to her own death. Actually, this is the case for Locke regardless of a person's age. In his brief discussion of suicide in Chapter IV on Slavery, Locke suggests that it would only ever be possible for an individual to alienate his right to life under circumstances in which continuing to live would be so miserable

---

support this claim, he cites God's patient treatment of the Israelites in the Old Testament.

that death would come as a great relief (*2T* 23). This is clearly not the sort of consideration on the table for Jephthah's daughter, who is so fond of her life and its potential that she asks for time to grieve her own lost future before meeting her fate.

§3. The Puzzle: Why Jephthah?

By this point, I hope to have demonstrated at least the modest claim that, as a whole, the Jephthah story is deeply problematic from the standpoint of Lockean principles. But this in itself does not necessarily prove that Locke's *use* of Jephthah is problematic, or that it should call into question any of his teachings related to "Appealing to Heaven," conscience or resistance. For, one might argue that Locke uses the isolated moment of Jephthah's "Appeal to Heaven" without being aware or concerned with the problems involved in the larger story (although, as we have seen, even Jephthah's "appeal" is independently problematic). I think it is highly unlikely that Locke was unaware of the Jephthah story as a whole; it is generally accepted that Locke was a serious student of the Bible, and the fact that he provides some background information about Jephthah when he mentions him in 109 of the *Second Treatise* suggests that he is aware of the story in its context.[34]

Still, the case might be made that Locke simply references the Jephthah story selectively, isolating the part of the story that supports his argument with no expectation that his omission of the rest will pose any problem or provoke any suspicion in his audience. This is roughly the position taken by Samuel Moyn, who argues that Locke's sole interest in the Jephthah story is to support his view on the existence of norms amidst anarchy, and that "there was no need for Locke's political theory to follow the details of the Jephthah story in other particulars."[35] Although I ultimately disagree with Moyn, I take his position seriously because I am compelled by

---

[34] In *2T* 109, Locke explains that the Gileadites sought Jephthah out to "article with him" after having previously banished him for being a "bastard."

[35] Moyn, "Appealing to Heaven," 286.

the reasoning he gives in support of it: Moyn makes the historical claim that, in highlighting only Jephthah's "colloquy" with the Ammonites and ignoring the filicide, Locke "fits within a tradition of Protestant invocations of the story."[36] I think Moyn's interest in the then-contemporary status of the story is valid, and I agree that the way in which a biblical story has historically been received is certainly relevant when attempting to determine an author's intention in citing that story. I grant, if it *were* true that, at the time Locke wrote the *Second Treatise,* Jephthah was an obscure figure known only for his diplomatic mission, then I would be more willing to dismiss Jephthah's overall inappropriateness for Locke's teaching. However, in the present section of this chapter I aim to show that this was not indeed the case. On the contrary, the Jephthah story—*especially* the vow and filicide— had been the subject of a rich history of exegesis, religious reflection, and literary adaptation. It is hard to imagine that Locke's readers would have heard the name Jephthah without first thinking of his crime. ·

§3.1. Jephthah, the Diplomat, in Locke's Close Contemporaries: Milton, Grotius, and Sidney. First, I will concede to Moyn that, in the selective examples of Jephthah "invocations" he cites—namely, those made by John Milton and (with greater stress) Hugo Grotius—it is true that Jephthah is mentioned only in relation to his diplomatic attempt, and without reference to any other part of his story. In his poem *Samson Agonistes* (1671), Milton makes a passing reference to Jephthah in which he alludes only to Jephthah's pre-battle dialogue with the Ammonites: "*Jephthah,* who by argument, / Not worse than by his shield and spear / Defended *Israel* from the *Ammonite.*"[37] Even more promising for Moyn's argument is Grotius' reference to Jephthah in *Rights of War and Peace* (1625). Grotius uses the Jephthah story to show that even when God does not provide a direct

---

[36] Moyn,"Appealing to Heaven," 286.

[37] John Milton, "Samson Agonistes," The John Milton Reading Room, Dartmouth University, Accessed February 24, 2021. https://www.dartmouth.edu/~milton/reading_room/samson/drama/text.shtml

"warrant," there are just reasons for going to war that can be discovered by the "Light of Nature."[38] According to Moyn, Locke is closely following Grotius in using Jephthah as an example of the persistence of norms even in conditions of anarchy.[39]

Admittedly, Moyn might have further supported his argument by citing the Jephthah references made by a writer in much closer proximity to Locke—namely, Algernon Sidney. Sidney composed his *Discourses Concerning Government* at roughly the same time Locke wrote the *Second Treatise*, and for arguably the same purpose. As Richard Ashcraft has provocatively demonstrated, Locke and Sidney were both involved (though in varying degrees) in a circle of revolutionaries led by their mutual acquaintance, the Earl of Shaftesbury, who had radical plans for resistance long before the Glorious Revolution took place.[40] Along with a few other "literary" representatives of this group, Locke and Sidney both produced works (the *Second Treatise* and the *Discourses* respectively) that were meant to provide a philosophical justification for the impending acts of resistance. Interestingly, Ashcraft has shown that most of these works engaged in a shared "code" language in which (for instance): arguments for the proper "end" of government were made through reference to a state of nature; government abuse of trust was characterized in terms of "invasion," "rebellion," or facilitating a "state of war" with the people; and the princes who did so were described in

---

[38] Hugo Grotius, *The Rights of War and Peace*, ed. by Richard Tuck (Indianapolis: Liberty Fund, 2005), 187.

[39] Moyn, "Appealing to Heaven," 294.

[40] Richard Ashcraft, "Revolutionary Politics and Locke's Two Treatises of Government: Radicalism and Lockean Political Theory," *Political Theory*, vol. 8, no. 4 (Nov. 1980): 429–486. Ashcraft goes so far as to suggest that Shaftesbury (and by extension Locke) was involved in the "Rye House Plot" to assassinate Charles II and his brother James, Duke of York in order to ensure that a Catholic did not take the throne. While Locke's role in the "Rye House Plot" is unclear, it is generally agreed that Locke indeed wrote the *Second Treatise* in anticipation of, rather than as a retroactive justification for, the revolutionary events preceding the Glorious Revolution.

animal terms similar to those used by Locke.[41] Sidney's *Discourses* has the added familiarity of being formally composed (and far more systematically than in Locke's *Two Treatises*) as a refutation of Filmer. Given this practice of "shared language" and shared aims, it is therefore extremely striking that Sidney also mentions Jephthah in his *Discourses*—and no fewer than seven times.[42] Sidney's use of Jephthah is varied, and often Jephthah's name just appears in a litany of Old Testament figures meant to serve as some kind of counterexample to one of Filmer's claims. Still, it is remarkable that not one of Sidney's seven references to Jephthah even hints at the filicide. Was Locke simply "on trend" in referencing Jephthah in such a selective way? In order to answer this question, we need to consider the fuller picture of Jephthah's cultural significance.

§3.2. Jephthah's "Rash" Vow, Through the Ages. Milton, Grotius, and Sidney may have cited Jephthah without reference to his vow or filicide, but in doing so they were outliers in the history of Jephthah commentary. Beginning in the first century (as far as we know), readers of the Jephthah story have focused almost exclusively on the vow and filicide. At various points in the history of this commentary there have been attempts to domesticate the vow by providing an alternate ending in which (usually) Jephthah consecrates his daughter to a life of chastity instead of sacrificing her.[43] But for the most

---

[41] Ashcraft, "Revolutionary Politics," 466–475.

[42] Algernon Sidney, *Discourses Concerning Government*, ed. by Thomas G. West (Indianapolis, IN: Liberty Fund, 1996). Sidney's references to Jephthah occur at: I.3, II.9, II.24, II.32, III.1, III.31, and III.39.

[43] For the alternate endings posited by medieval Jewish scholars Joseph and David Kimhi, see Anna Linton, "Sacrificed or Spared? The Fate of Jephthah's Daughter in Early Modern Theological and Literary Texts," *German Life and Letters*, 57: 3 (July 2004): 240. For discussion of treatment given by early Christian writer Nicholas of Lyra, see Thompson 151–152, and N. Scott Amos, "'Do to Me According to What Has Gone Out of Your Mouth:' A Reformation Debate on the Tragedy of Jephthah and his Daughter," *Reformation & Renaissance Review: Journal of the Society for Reformation Studies*, vol. 21, no.1 (2019): 3–26. The consecration-to-

part, readers have accepted the view that Jephthah goes through with the sacrifice, and their preoccupation has generally been to wrestle with why he does so, and why God allows it. It is beyond the scope of this chapter to give a full gloss on the fascinating history of this commentary, and excellent work on that project has already been done.[44] But I would like to give a brief survey of some of the prominent strands of Jephthah commentary, especially from those writers Locke and his readers would have been most likely to have encountered.

In most of the early Jewish and Christian commentary, Jephthah was condemned not only for the filicide, but for making such a foolish vow in the first place. Some commentators went so far as to say that God allows Jephthah to go through with the sacrifice (instead of intervening, as he did for Abraham and Isaac) in order to punish Jephthah for making the vow,[45] or as a warning to others against making rash vows.[46] As St. Augustine stresses, unlike Abraham—who acts in accordance with a *mandate* from God—Jephthah acts in accordance with his own spontaneous vow, which God never

---

virginity ending was also revived by some writers in the seventeenth century; it is put forth, for example, in John Downame's *Annotations* (1645) and Sir Thomas Browne's *Pseudodoxia Epidemica* (1646). For citation and discussion, see Marjorie Swann, "Marriage, Celibacy, and Ritual in Robert Herrick's *Hesperides*," *Philological Quarterly*, vol. 76:1 (1997): 19f.

[44] One of the earliest and most notable studies in the field of comparative literature was published by W. O. Sypherd, *Jephthah and his Daughter: A Study in Comparative Literature* (Newark: University of Delaware, 1948). Other works in comparative literature I have found very helpful in researching this chapter are: Mary Nyquist, "The Plight of Jephthah's Daughter: Sacrifice, Sovereignty, and Paternal Power," *Comparative Literature*, vol. 60, no. 4 (2008): 331–354, and Bernard Robinson, "The Story of Jephthah and his Daughter" (2004). An excellent work in historical theology on which I have relied heavily in my research is John L. Thompson, *Writing the Wrongs* (Oxford University Press, 2001).

[45] Pseudo-Philo, *Biblical Antiquities,* as cited in Thompson, *Writing the Wrongs,* 108.

[46] For an example of this reading, see John Chrysostom, as cited in Thompson, *Writing the Wrongs,* 117.

sanctions.[47] Condemnation of Jephthah's vow continued into the medieval period, where Thomas Aquinas presented it as an example of a vow that should not have been observed, citing with approval St. Jerome's verdict that "In vowing, he was foolish because he did not use discretion, and in keeping the vow he was impious."[48] In Peter Abelard's poetic dramatization of the story, Jephthah's daughter is lauded as a heroine, while Jephthah is an "enemy of his kin," overtaken by the "mad zeal of a prince."[49]

The emphasis on the rashness of Jephthah's vow received a renewed interest in the sixteenth century, where it began to play a role in Reformation polemics.[50] Martin Luther harshly indicted the vow as being both foolish and superstitious.[51] In a similar vein—but closer to home for Locke's audience—was the more extensive commentary on Jephthah given by John Calvin, who cited the story at least five separate times. Calvin used Jephthah as a means for reflection on vowing in general, which he deemed a form of "willworship" and "private madnesse."[52] Importantly for our purposes, Calvin's views on Jephthah should have been commonly known to the English people of the time because, as Mary Nyquist explains, they were

---

[47] Augustine takes Pseudo-Philo's reading in an even darker direction, suggesting that Jephthah secretly had his wife in mind when making the vow, and that God sends his daughter out first instead as a punishment. Augustine, *"Questiones in Heptateuchum,"* 7.49.6–7.49.7, as cited and discussed in N. Scott Amos, 2019.

[48] For more discussion on Jerome (347–419) and his commentary on Jephthah, see Thompson, 120f.

[49] Abelard, *Planctus Virginum Israel Super filia Jeptae Galditae, (Lament of the Virgins of Israel over the Daughter of Jephthah the Gileadite)*, translated by Philo M. Buck, University of Wisconsin, and reprinted in Sypherd, *Jephthah and his Daughter*, 8–10.

[50] Specifically, in the debate over the validity of religious vows in general, a question of controversy between Protestants and Roman Catholics. For a discussion of this debate, see Anna Linton, "Sacrificed or Spared?", 242f.

[51] As cited in Thompson, *Writing the Wrongs*, 155.

[52] From Folio 83; 4, 13, 1. As cited and discussed in Nyquist, "The Plight of Jephthah's Daughter," 343.

adapted and widely distributed in the form of the 1547 homily "Against Swearing and Perjury."[53] Here, notably, Jephthah's vow was condemned as being "against God's eternal will and the Lawe of Nature."[54]

This theme of Jephthah's vow being in conflict with Natural Law was taken up most forcefully in the tragic adaptation of the story by Scottish playwright and philosopher George Buchanan, *Iepthes Sive Votum* (1554).[55] Buchanan invents several characters—a Priest, and Jephthah's wife, whom he names "Storge"—who attempt to dissuade Jephthah from going through with his vow on the grounds that there is never a moral obligation to commit evil: God would never command something that goes against his own Natural Laws.[56] The Priest emphasizes that God manifests these laws to us through our natural inclinations, chief of which is a parent's love for his children.[57] Adding to this Lockean train of thought is Storge,

---

[53] "Against Swearing" (whose author is unknown, but possibly Archbishop Cranmer) appeared in the volume *Certayne Sermons, or homelies*, a collection commissioned by King Edward VI, with the intention that the contents be preached from pulpits across the country. For the text of this volume, see Ronald Bond, *Certain Sermons or Homilies (1547) and A Homily against Disobedience and Wilful Rebellion (1570): A Critical Edition* (Toronto: University of Toronto Press, 1987).

[54] Quotation from Bond edition, as cited in Marjorie Swann, "Marriage, Celibacy and Ritual."

[55] Citations refer to the English translation of the play by P. G. Walsh in *George Buchanan Tragedies,* ed. P. Sharratt and P. G. Walsh (Edinburgh: Scottish Academic Press, 1983). For extensive discussion and comparative study of the play, see Nyquist, "The Plight of Jephthah's Daughter," 331–354.

[56] Jephthah insists that by granting him victory, God had signaled his sanction of the vow, and his expectation that Jephthah go through with it: "my victory attests that mine [my vow] was welcome" (Buchanan, *Iepthes*, 88).

[57] "How is it open to you to carry through what our sacred mother nature forbids, what our love of kin struggles against, and what God loathes? Nature has implanted in our emotions the love of children first and foremost" (Buchanan, *Iepthes,* 81–82).

who forcefully objects to Jephthah's planned filicide in part by arguing that mothers have an equal share in parental right: "She is a
shared pledge of love," Storge says, in reference to their daughter, as
she insists that both parents must have a say in the fate of their children.[58] Storge's argument is strikingly resonant of Locke's own
theory of "*parental* right," which he takes great pains to distinguish
from "*paternal* right" by emphasizing its inclusion of the mother.[59]
This is just a sampling of the ways in which Buchanan's adaptation
of the Jephthah story masterfully exposes many of the problems the
narrative *should* pose for Locke: Jephthah's violation of natural law,
parental tenderness as an indication of God's will, and even the
equal right of mothers. And it is reasonable to assume that Locke
and his audience would have been familiar with Buchanan's retelling
of the story. Today Buchanan is best known for his political writings,[60] but according to Nyquist, during the sixteenth and seventeenth centuries he was also "widely regarded as western Europe's
pre-eminent Latin poet." It is likely that Locke and his audience
would have been familiar with Buchanan's work, both political and
poetic.[61]

Indeed, the Jephthah story—in its entirety—became increasingly mainstream in the sixteenth and seventeenth centuries, as it
even found its way into some of the popular folk ballads of the time,
including one that is briefly quoted in Shakespeare's *Hamlet*.[62] In

---

[58] Buchanan, *Iepthes*, 88.

[59] In the *First Treatise*, Locke often reminds Filmer that the full
commandment is "honor your Father *and* Mother," and that the power
parents have over their children is a shared one (*1T* 8, 55, 63). In the *Second Treatise*, Locke continues to insist on shared parental power, strength-
ening the basis for his claim regarding the rights of mothers: "If we consult
Reason or Revelation we shall find she hath an equal title" (*2T* 52).

[60] Coincidentally, he was also the author of a 1579 treatise justifying
political resistance, *De Juro Regnia apud Scotos Dialogues*, or "*A Dialogue on
the Law of Kingship Amongst the Scots*."

[61] Nyquist, "The Plight of Jephthah's Daughter," 332.

[62] Sypherd, *Jephthah and his Daughter*, 12. The ballad appears in
Hamlet II.2.405–422.

1649, one of Locke's close contemporaries, Robert Herrick, published a poem called "The Dirge for Jephthah's Daughter," which (unlike Milton's *Samson Agonistes*) emphasizes the filicide.[63] Though the speakers of the poem acknowledge Jephthah's victory over the Ammonites and the "liberty" it bought for them, they insist that it was not worth the price Jephthah's daughter had to pay for it: "And in the purchase of our peace, / The cure was worse than the disease."[64]

Finally, there is the reference to Jephthah's filicide made by none other than Locke's antithesis, Thomas Hobbes, who cites Jephthah in one of the most infamous chapters of the *Leviathan*, "Of the Liberty of Subjects."[65] Here Hobbes presents the story of Jephthah and his daughter (in conjunction with the story of David and Uriah) in support of his fascinating dual thesis that, while it *is* possible for the sovereign to violate the laws of nature and of God (including by punishing an innocent subject), in doing so the sovereign commits only a sin against God/nature, *not* an "injury" or "injustice" against the subject.[66] Thus, while Hobbes uses Jephthah as

---

[63] As cited in the *Hesperides & Noble Numbers* volume edited by Alfred Pollard. For commentary on Herrick's "Dirge," see Marjorie Swann, "Marriage, Celibacy, and Ritual," 19.

[64] Herrick, "Dirge," line 25–30.

[65] In addition to his more memorable reference to Jephthah in Chapter XXI, Hobbes also briefly mentions Jephthah as an example to illustrate the metaphorical significance of phrases such as "spirit," or "angel." According to Hobbes, when the Scripture tells us that "the spirit of the Lord was upon Jephthah" it really just means that Jephthah was overcome by extraordinary zeal and courage (Hobbes, *Leviathan*, 294).

[66] The passage reads as follows: "And therefore it may (and doth often) happen in commonwealths that a subject may be put to death by the command of the sovereign power, and yet neither do the other wrong, as when Jephthah caused his daughter to be sacrificed (in which, and in like cases, he that so dieth had liberty to do the action for which he is nevertheless without injury put to death). And the same holdeth also in a sovereign prince that putteth to death an innocent subject. For though the action be against the law of nature, as being contrary to equity, (as was the

an example to support his view of absolute and arbitrary power, he implicitly admits that Jephthah sins against God and the laws of nature. (From a Lockean standpoint, this means that while Jephthah might be in the clear from the standpoint of human judgment, he will be in trouble on that "last day.") Bizarrely, for Hobbes, the Jephthah story also has the added benefit of providing an example of a subject—the daughter—who, while innocent, nevertheless had the "liberty" to do the action for which she is put to death (presumably, Hobbes means her action of walking out of the house first). But this only makes sense under Hobbes's notoriously narrow definition of "liberty," and, as we have seen, there is no sense in which Jephthah's daughter can be understood to "consent" according to Lockean principles. In sum, that Locke's adversary cites Jephthah in order to *support* arguments antithetical to Locke's own project—while, at the same time, directly illuminating what *should* be, for Locke, the problematic aspects of the story—only intensifies the mystery as to why Locke cites Jephthah without any reference to his crime.[67]

§3.3. Can we Separate Jephthah's "Vow" from his "Appeal"? To conclude this section, I hope to have demonstrated by this point that, despite the outliers discussed in §3.1, the most familiar aspect of the Jephthah story for Locke and his audience would have still been Jephthah's fateful vow and filicide. But even more important than the dramatic link between Jephthah's "appeal" and his "vow" is the conceptual link between these two acts, which is especially obvious in Locke's invocation of Jephthah as a model for "Appealing to Heaven," and all that entails regarding "confidence of conscience." Recall that, for Locke, appealing to heaven means not only having

---

killing of Uriah) yet it was not an injury to Uriah, but to God" (Hobbes, *Leviathan*, 131).

[67] For excellent comparative discussions of Hobbes's and Locke's respective references to Jephthah, see Jonathan Sheehan, "Assenting to the Law: Sacrifice and Punishment at the Dawn of Secularism," in *After Secular Law*, ed. by Winnifred Fallers Sullivan, Robert A. Yelle, and Mateo Taussig-Rubbo (Stanford: Stanford University Press, 2011), 62–79; and Arthur Bradley, "Let the Lord the Judge be Judge," 1–20.

confidence that one has "right" on one's side, but also that the potential costs and consequences of the appeal are worth its pursuit. In some sense, Jephthah's sacrifice of his daughter can be characterized as a "result"—though tragically unforeseen—of his Appeal. Apparently, he was not quite confident enough in the Gileadites' ability to defeat the Ammonites by their own merits, and felt he had to obtain extra help from God through what was essentially a bribe.[68] Thus, in a way, his "vow," and by extension his daughter's death, can be said to be an auxiliary means to fulfilling his appeal. Indeed, in both Buchanan's play and Herrick's poem, her death is characterized as the direct "price" of the victory over the Ammonites.[69] Perhaps Jephthah is Locke's way of warning a potential "Appealer" that it is impossible to foresee all of the possible consequences of one's actions.

§4. Closing Remarks

On that note, I will close by saying a few words about what I think is obvious about Locke's use of Jephthah, as well as admitting what still remains obscure. I think it is obvious, though perhaps not immediately, that Locke's use of Jephthah is problematic; and I hope to have demonstrated that it is problematic in such a way that Locke could have reasonably expected his careful readers to be alarmed by it. In other words, Locke's use of Jephthah is both problematic and deliberate. What is less obvious, then, is *why* Locke chooses to use Jephthah—and, on this point, I am still working in the realm of hypothesis. My inclination, though, is to say that, through Jephthah, Locke signals a more cautious or conservative attitude towards re-

---

[68] This is indeed how many theologians read Jephthah's vow. Daniel Block, for example, characterizes Jephthah as a pagan attempting to manipulate God. His was a "deadly serious expression of devotion"—an attempt to try to win favor as one would with a pagan God. Daniel Block, *Judges, Ruth: An Exegetical and Theological Exposition of Holy Scripture* (Nashville: Broadman and Holman, 1999), 367.

[69] In Buchanan's play, Jephthah even goes so far as to beg God to rescind his victory so that he does not have to go through with the sacrifice (Buchanan, *Iepthes*, 79).

sistance than is usually attributed to him. Locke introduces Jephthah as a model of someone who "appeals to Heaven," but Jephthah turns out to be someone whose mistaken "confidence in conscience" ends up producing disastrous results. Surely, Locke must have witnessed similar lapses of judgment made on the pretense of conscience in his own time, living through the English Civil War and its aftermath—he tells us as much in his *Two Tracts*. To view Jephthah as a kind of "moderating device" would therefore also help us reconcile Locke's teaching on the right of resistance in the *Second Treatise* with some of his earlier skepticism about "conscience," and with his profound anxieties about epistemic anarchy. Perhaps Locke never fully outgrew those anxieties, but only gave them a subtler expression in his more mature writings.

Admittedly, though, this view seems to go against the more intuitive assumption that a philosopher might use textual devises in order to conceal the more *radical* aspects of his teachings, not the reverse.[70] If I am correct that Locke still retains some more conservative anxieties about resistance, why would he go to the trouble of concealing them beneath a dangerously radical veneer? Though not completely satisfying, here Ashcraft's thesis on the empirical conditions under which Locke composed the *Second Treatise* might point toward a more promising answer. As discussed briefly above, Ashcraft contends that Locke was part of a literary circle whose task—as apparently commissioned by the Earl of Shaftesbury—was to provide a philosophical defense of their impending acts of resistance. The "shared language" used in this circle often included claims of "invasions" against not only the property, lives and liberties of the subjects (the Lockean trinity), but also against their *consciences*.[71] And as we have seen, at least one other person in this circle (Algernon Sidney) references Jephthah as an example of a "liberator"

---

[70] See, for instance, Leo Strauss, *Persecution and the Art of Writing* (Glencoe, Illinois: Free Press, 1952).

[71] See Ashcraft, "Revolutionary Politics," 470. There's some evidence that Locke himself absorbed this language in *2T* 209, where, in addition to naming the usual trinity he mentions that the people will appeal to heaven when they feel that "perhaps their religion too" is in danger.

without any reference to his crime. Is it possible that by including a more subtle and provocative reference to Jephthah, Locke signals his distance from, and reservations about, the radical project to which he had been invited to contribute?

LOCKE'S REVOLUTION IN THE "LAW OF FASHION"

J. Judd Owen

The principal spring from which the actions of men take their rise, the rule they conduct them by, and the end to which they direct them, seems to be credit and reputation, and that which at any rate they avoid, is in the greatest part shame and disgrace....He therefore that would govern the world well, had need consider rather what fashions he makes, than what laws; and to bring anything into use he need only give it reputation. (Locke's journal entry; December 12, 1678)

John Locke is rightly regarded as one of the principal architects of the revolution in political thought that came to be known as liberalism, with its emphasis on toleration, individual rights, limited government based on consent, and, at least until fairly recently, rationalism. At the center of the study of Locke's political thought is his teaching on government and what he called *civil law*, particularly at the foundational or constitutional level. Scholars of his political thought have also paid much attention to the place in it of *natural law*, which is no longer much associated with liberalism. Very little attention has been paid to what Locke alternately called the law of opinion, reputation, or fashion. The neglect of the law of fashion might be surprising in light of the fact that, in his most systematic treatment of "the true nature of law," he asserted that it is a far more effective form of law than either civil law or divine law, which includes natural law. Indeed, he supposed that "the greatest part" of mankind "govern themselves chiefly, if not solely, by this law of fashion."[1] This neglect is less surprising in light of the fact that his comments on the nature of law and the law of fashion occur, not in one of his political works proper, but deep in his famously daunting work on epistemology, the *Essay Concerning Human Understanding*. Indeed, the law of fashion makes no appearance in his political works, not at any rate as law. Moreover, it is not readily apparent how his comments on the law of fashion can be squared with what seems to be the core teaching of the *Second Treatise of Government*, viz. that the origin and purpose of government lies in an "original compact" among free and independent individuals fleeing the dangers endemic in the state of nature. Nevertheless, the law of fashion does, in fact, resonate throughout Locke's works, not only elsewhere in the *Essay*, but also especially in *Some Thoughts Concerning Education* and *Of the Conduct of the Understanding*.[2] Following these connections transforms our understanding of Locke's project, which aimed to be a revolution primarily in the law of fashion and only secondarily in civil law or government.

Locke's account of "the true nature of law" is the core of his account of "moral relations," which concern "the conformity or disagreement men's voluntary actions have to a rule, to which they are referred, and by which they are judged" (*ECHU* 2.28.4). Locke calls these rules laws. The account of law deep in Book 2 thus must be understood in light of his famous refutation, near the beginning of the *Essay*, of the claim that human beings possess an innate awareness of moral principles, including moral rules. In the course of that refutation, Locke time and again appeals to the great variety of moral principles from society to society—what he will identify in his account of law in Book 2 with the law of fashion:

---

[1] Locke, *An Essay Concerning Human Understanding*, ed. Peter H. Nidditch (Oxford: Clarendon Press, 1975), 2.28.6, 12. Hereafter cited as *ECHU* by book, chapter, and section.

[2] Locke, *Some Thoughts Concerning Education* and *Of the Conduct of the Understanding*, ed. Ruth W. Grant and Nathan Tarcov (Indianapolis: Hackett, 1996). Hereafter cited as *STCE* and *CU* by section.

He that will carefully peruse the history of mankind and look abroad into the several tribes of men, and with indifference survey their actions, will be able to satisfy himself that there is scarce that principle of morality to be named, or rule of virtue to be thought on...which is not somewhere or other slighted and condemned by the general fashion of whole societies of men, governed by practical opinions and rules of living quite opposite to others. (*ECHU* 1.3.10)

So far are human beings from having innate knowledge of moral principles that their minds begin, as Locke famously claims, as "white paper" capable of receiving "any characters" imprinted on them (*ECHU* 1.3.22). These "characters" come from one's "education and the fashions of his country" (*ECHU* 1.3.26). They may originate from nothing more than "the superstition of a nurse or the authority of an old woman, [and] may, by length of time, and consent of neighbors, grow up to the dignity of principles in religion and morality" (*ECHU* 1.3.22).

Locke stresses that, in denying that moral principles are innate, he is not thereby denying that there are in fact moral principles or that their truth can be known with certainty; just as the truth that the angles of a triangle equal two right angles is no less certain for not being innately known (*ECHU* 1.3.1). He thus associates true moral principles with natural law, discoverable by reason alone, "i.e., without the help of positive revelation" (*ECHU* 1.3.13): "For God...by an inseparable connection joined virtue and public happiness together and made the practice thereof necessary to the preservation of society and visibly beneficial to all" (*ECHU* 1.3.6). Nevertheless, awareness of the "several moral rules" that are beneficial for society, however universally acknowledged those rules may be, does not amount to full knowledge of them as true moral rules. For "the true ground of morality...can only be the will and law of a God, who sees men in the dark, has in his hands rewards and punishments, and power enough to call to account the proudest offender" (*ECHU* 1.3.6). As we will see, rules alone are not enough. Those rules must be issued by one with authority to do so and, what is no less important, with the power to enforce them. Whether reason alone can discover the source (God as law-giver) and enforcement of the true moral law, or only the rules themselves, is unclear. At this stage it seems clear that only divine law is true moral law.

The question, indeed the problem,[3] of moral rules having been established early in the *Essay*, one could hardly be expected to guess from the table of contents where or even that Locke returns to the question by defining and classifying moral rules, now identified with "the nature of law, properly so called." The account of the nature of law and of the surprisingly important law of fashion could almost be considered hidden, as it occurs in the very middle of the *Essay*, some pages into Book 2 chapter 28, the title of which, "Of other Relations," offers no clue as to the moral and political importance of its contents. Book 2 of the *Essay* comprises an extended account of the origin and types of "ideas" that are the stuff of all human thought—the characters that come to be stamped on the white paper of the mind, coming first from sense perception, then from reflection. "Of other Relations" is the fourth in a series of chapters on those ideas that enter the mind through the comparison of ideas. These relational ideas include cause and effect (*ECHU* 2.26), identity and diversity (*ECHU* 2.27), and, as he says in chapter 28, "infinite others," such as those concerning parts, degrees, equality, and excess; as well as "natural relations," such as father and son.

Next and broaching the question of morality just before turning to law, are relations that entail "a moral right, power, or obligation to do something," such as between general and army (*ECHU* 2.28.3). Relations of moral right, power, and obligation—"*all this sort* depend[] upon men's wills, or agreement in society" (emphasis added). All moral authority is "instituted, or voluntary; and may be distinguished from the natural" (*ECHU* 2.28.3). Father has no natural moral authority over son; that authority is instituted by human will. This account reflects the teaching of the *Second Treatise of*

---

[3] Cf. J. Judd Owen, *Making Religion Safe for Democracy: Transformation from Hobbes to Tocqueville* (New York: Cambridge University Press, 2015), 91–97.

Government regarding the role of consent in establishing parental and political authority.[4] It seems, however, to contradict what he had said in Book 1 about the "true ground of morality" being only the will and law of a God.[5]

Having established the basis of the right one (human being) has to direct the actions of another and the corresponding obligation to obey, Locke arrives at the rules themselves that direct action on that basis: what he calls ideas of "moral relations." Although moral relations appear far down the chain of ideas viewed from a purely epistemological point of view, they are nevertheless of the utmost importance for human beings. For it is not enough to have a clearly determined idea of the various sorts of human action, in terms of their "ends, objects, manners, and circumstances." Our *greatest* concern, Locke says, is in determining whether our actions are "*morally good or bad*" (*ECHU* 2.28.4, emphasis added). In order to understand what it means for an action to be morally good or bad, it is necessary first to understand what good and bad mean most basically. Locke uses "bad" and "evil" synonymously, claiming to have previously shown that "good and evil...are nothing but pleasure and pain," and what are conducive of pleasure and pain, including both sensations of the body and perceptions of the mind (*ECHU* 2.28.5; cf. 2.20.1–2). Good and evil are most basically *amoral* ideas; *moral* good and evil being a subclass of good and evil, or pleasure and pain, generally. Moral good and evil stems from the "conformity or disagreement of our voluntary actions to some law, *whereby good or evil*

---

[4] Locke, *Two Treatises of Government*, ed. Peter Laslett (New York: Cambridge University Press, 1960) 74–75, 95, 110, 119. Hereafter cited as *2T* by section.

[5] "We call a positive consensus one which issues from a compact, either tacit, as when some common human necessity or advantage draws men to it,...or express...Neither of these kinds of agreements proves the existence of a law of nature at all, since they both depend entirely on a compact, and issue from no principle of nature whatsoever" (Locke, *Questions Concerning the Law of Nature*, ed. and tr. Robert Horwitz, Jenny Strauss Clay, and Diskin Clay [Ithaca, NY: Cornell University Press], 175).

is drawn on us, from the will and power of the law-maker, which good and evil, pleasure or pain, attending our observance, or breach of the law, by the decree of the law-maker is that we call reward and punishment" (*ECHU* 2.28.5, emphasis added). No action is, then, inherently morally good or evil. Nor is an action good (pleasant) or evil (painful) simply through the adherence or violation of the law-maker's decree. Such an action is made good (pleasant) or evil (painful) through reward or punishment "annexed to that law."

Accordingly, moral good and evil do not refer to the "natural product and consequence of an action," since the pleasure and pain that follow naturally from an action affect behavior without need for a law. Reward and punishment apart from natural consequences are thus essential to moral good and evil, "since it would be utterly in vain to suppose a rule set to the free actions of man without annexing to it some enforcement of good and evil to determine his will." The law-giver accordingly needs *power*, the "power to reward the compliance with and punish the deviation from his rule" (*ECHU* 2.28.6). Thus "the nature of law, properly so called" entails one intelligent being directing the will of another through rules by way of the power of enforcement.

Following this definition, Locke identifies three sorts of law. First on Locke's list is divine law, which is the law by which God directs human actions, and it can be promulgated by either "the light of nature or the voice of revelation" (*ECHU* 2.28.8). His previous denial that the true moral law can be known only through revelation is not a denial of revelation. Rather, true revelation would serve either to confirm the principles that reason can discover on its own, i.e. natural law, or to allow the natural law to be recognized by those without the capacity to discern it for themselves.[6] The second sort of law is civil law, which is "the rule set by the commonwealth" for the protection of "the lives, liberties, and possessions of those who live according to its laws" (*ECHU* 2.28.9). Readers of Locke's

---

[6] Cf. Locke, *The Reasonableness of Christianity*, ed. John C. Higgins-Biddle (New York: Oxford University Press, 1999), 241–243, hereafter cited as *RC* by section number; *ECHU* 4.17. 23–24.

political works have some familiarity with the first two sorts of law, but not with the third—at least not as law. And he seems a bit uncertain even what to call it: "the law of opinion, or reputation, if I may so call it," later and more consistently calling it the law of fashion. The terms we attach to compliance or violation of the law of fashion, however, are as familiar as those with regard to the other sorts of law: "By the relation they bear to the first of these [divine law], men judge whether their actions are sins or duties; by the second [civil law], whether they be criminal or innocent; and by the third [the law of fashion], whether they be virtues or vices" (*ECHU* 2.28.7). Judgments of virtue and vice are commonplace, but the sort of law that designates virtue and vice, as distinguished from divine and civil law, has no common name.

What seems at first a fairly straightforward, if unconventional, classification of law, presents a number of perplexities upon examination. Do all of the three sorts of law Locke enumerates meet the definition he had just offered? Do fashion and reputation in particular warrant being called law? Locke himself anticipates such an objection with regard to the law of fashion, saying that someone might "imagine that I have forgotten my own notion of a law when I make the law whereby men judge of virtue and vice to be nothing else but the consent of private men, who have not authority enough to make a law: especially wanting that which is so necessary and essential to law, a power to enforce it" (*ECHU* 2.28.12). This hypothetical objection raises two questions: one with regard to the grounds of the authority of the law-giver, and another with regard to the power of enforcement. Now, earlier it had been unclear whether Locke considered the ground of authority of the law-giver to be part of the definition of law, as it appears just prior to his account of "moral relations," which he identifies with law. This is significant because, as we noted above, he provides two different accounts of the ground of moral authority: the one saying it can only be God, in which case only divine law is true law; the other saying that moral authority is instituted by the will of human beings, i.e. consent. The "true nature of law properly so-called" includes *both* divine and human law. He now confirms that the ground of authority is indeed part of his "own notion of a law," but he does not respond to the question about the ground of authority of the law of fashion, coming around to say only that it "by a secret and tacit consent establishes itself in the several societies, tribes, and clubs of men in the world" (*ECHU* 2.28.12). The role of consent in establishing moral authority appears to be confirmed, but he says nothing about who the law-giver(s) of fashion are whose authority is thus established. Can one consent, even tacitly, to a law whose origin is uncertain or mistaken? It thus remains unclear whether the law of fashion is true law properly so called.[7]

With regard to the second question regarding enforcement of the law of fashion, however—the essential importance of which he underscores—his answer is emphatic. Those who fail to recognize the degree to which human beings conform their behavior according to the reward and punishment of praise and censure of those around them "seem[] little skilled in the nature or history of mankind, the greatest part whereof he shall find to govern themselves chiefly, if not solely, by this law of fashion" (*ECHU* 2.28.12). Indeed, as far as enforcement is concerned, the law of fashion is far more effective than either divine law or civil law:

> The penalties that attend the breach of God's laws, some, nay, perhaps most men seldom seriously reflect on: and among those that do, many, while they break the law, entertain thoughts of future reconciliation and making their peace for such breaches. And as to the punishments due from the laws of the commonwealth, they frequently flatter themselves with the hope of impunity. But no man es-

---

[7]Cf. *Questions*, p. 159. Note that in the epigraph above, although admittedly from a journal entry several years prior to writing the *Essay*, Locke distinguishes fashion from law. See also Locke's first note to *ECHU* 2.28.11, where he says that in that chapter he is "showing the original and nature of moral Ideas and enumerating the rules men make use of in moral relations, whether those rules be true or false." He thereby does not state "what I think of the eternal and unalterable nature of right and wrong"; instead, "I report as matters of fact what others call virtue and vice."

capes the punishment of their censure and dislike who offends against the fashion and opinion of the company he keeps and would recommend himself to....[N]o body, that has the least thought or sense of a man about him, can live in society under constant dislike and ill opinion of his familiars and those he converses with. (*ECHU* 2.28.12)[8]

Locke's merely partial response to the objections he anticipates indicates the paramount importance of enforcement—punishments and rewards—for his notion of law. That is, what appears to be of greater concern to Locke than the source of authority is the capacity of "law" to direct human behavior beyond, or even contrary to, natural consequences. He is above all concerned, in other words, with what Machiavelli calls the "effectual truth."[9] By that measure, the law of fashion is by far the most effective owing to the supreme effectiveness of its enforcement. Indeed, the effectiveness of the three sorts of law stand in inverse relation to the rank in authority of each law's source.

If Locke is indeed concerned principally with the "effectual truth," this could shed light on the apparent discrepancy noted above regarding the basis of moral authority. For Locke might suppose that the ground of the true moral law can only be the will of God and at the same time think that obligation comes into *effect* only through consent, either express or tacit, irrespective of any other claim with regard to the law-giver.

However that may be, as the importance of enforcement becomes clearer, this inverse ranking of authority and effectiveness raises questions about divine law. With regard to the law of nature, we might already have wondered how any law could be strictly natural when Locke made plain that natural consequences are not

---

[8] Cf. *Questions*, p. 111: "How rare is the man in the commonwealth who knows the laws of his city, which have been published, displayed in public places, easy to read and comprehend, and obvious to every eye? How much rarer is he who knows the hidden and unperceived laws of nature?"

[9] Niccolo Machiavelli, *The Prince*, tr. Harvey C. Mansfield (Chicago: University of Chicago Press) ch. 15.

properly considered rewards and punishments. Moral law requires rewards and punishments that are "annexed to" the law (*ECHU* 2.28.5). With regard to divine law as a whole, Locke says that God has "power to enforce [it] by rewards and punishments of infinite weight and duration in another life" (*ECHU* 2.28.8).[10] Although the content of natural law may be discoverable by reason alone, it is unclear how divine law could be fully natural in light of the means of enforcement, "which is so necessary and essential to a Law" (*ECHU* 2.28.12).[11]

If we stick to the "true nature of law, properly so called" and include in it the principle of consent, only civil law would appear to fit without qualification or unresolved questions. If, that is, we accept the teaching of the *Second Treatise*, we can say that the authority of the civil law-givers has been "instituted" by "men's wills, or the agreement of society." And, although the civil law is breached more frequently than the law of fashion, nevertheless "[t]his law nobody overlooks: the rewards and punishments that enforce it, being ready at hand and suitable to the power that makes it: which is the force of the commonwealth,...[which] has power to take away life, liberty, or goods, from him who disobeys" (*ECHU* 2.28.8). Each of the three sorts of law has a certain claim to primacy.

Returning to the law of fashion, it has two main parts. Most obviously identifiable with *fashion* is the part that varies from society to society, or from party to party within a society: "by the different temper, education, fashion, maxims, or interest of different sorts of

---

[10] "Nor is there any reason to be surprised at the diversity of men's opinions concerning what is right and virtuous given the fact that they disagree on even the most fundamental principles, and god and the immortality of the soul are called into doubt. These, although they are not practical propositions for the existence of natural law, must, nevertheless, be necessarily assumed for the existence of the law of nature, for there can be no law without a legislator and law will have no force if there is no punishment" (*Questions*, p. 193). Cf. *RC* 243.

[11] Cf. *ECHU* 4.3.27, 4.18.8; Leo Strauss, *Natural Right and History* (Chicago: University of Chicago Press, 1953), 212; and Owen 2015, 71–84.

men it fell out that what was thought praiseworthy in one place escaped not the censure in another; and so in different societies, virtues and vices were changed" (*ECHU* 2.28.11). The other part of the law of fashion is by and large the same everywhere, because "nothing can be more natural than to encourage with esteem and reputation that wherein everyone finds his advantage, and to blame and discountenance the contrary" (*ECHU* 2.28.11). As he had mentioned early in Book 1, there are certain rules of behavior whose social benefit is so visible to all human beings that both reason and their own interest direct them to praise and condemn accordingly, "few being depraved to that degree as not to condemn, at least in others, the faults they themselves are guilty of" (*ECHU* 2.28.11). In this way, "the true boundaries of the law of nature, which ought to be the rule of virtue and vice, were pretty well preserved" (*ECHU* 2.28.11). This leads, however, to another perplexity, as the law of nature now appears to fall into two columns, both as divine law and as law of fashion. But as we come increasingly to recognize the importance of enforcement for Locke's conception of law, we see which category of law is operative according to the means of enforcement—found in this case in esteem and reputation rather than the afterlife.

On the other hand, the law of fashion is surely not embraced by those subject to it as a law of *fashion*. Locke's identifying it with fashion is debunking, particularly with respect to that part that he does not associate with natural law. We can see more clearly what he has in mind when speaking of the law of fashion, and better appreciate its power, by returning to his refutation of innate moral principles early in the *Essay*, where he speaks of fashion imprinting characters on the naturally blank paper of the mind through education in childhood. This early imprinting forms the "basis and foundation on which [children] build their religion or manners [and] come, by these means to have the reputation of unquestionable, self-evident, and innate truth" (*ECHU* 1.3.22). Once grown to adulthood, they respect and submit to this received opinion, "not because it is [truly] natural...but because, having always been so educated, and having no remembrance of the beginning of this respect, they think it is natural" (*ECHU* 1.3.23). Indeed, more than natural, as this power, which Locke identifies with *custom*, "seldom fail[s] to make them worship for divine what [custom] hath inured them to bow their minds and submit their understandings to" (*ECHU* 1.3.25). When these ideas are then reinforced by the praise and censure of those around them, ·

> who dare venture to dissent from the received opinions of their country or party? And where is the man to be found, that can patiently prepare himself to bear the name of whimsical, sceptical, or atheist, which he is sure to meet with, who does in the least scruple any of the common opinions? And he will be much more afraid to question those principles, when he shall think them, as most men do, the standards set up by God in his mind, to be the rule and touchstone of all the other opinions. And what can hinder him from thinking them sacred, when he finds them the earliest of all his thoughts, and the most reverenced by others? (*ECHU* 1.3.25)

Locke symmetrically reiterates the point in the penultimate chapter of the *Essay*, again underscoring that the fashions or customs of the greatest concern are religious:

> There is nothing more ordinary than that children should receive into their minds propositions (*especially about matters of religion*) from their parents, nurses, or those about them, which being insinuated into their unwary, as well as unbiased understandings, and fastened by degrees, are at last (equally, whether true or false) riveted there by long custom and education beyond all possibility of being pulled out again. For men, when they are grown up, reflecting upon their opinions and finding those of this sort to be as ancient in their minds as their very memories, not having observed their early insinuation, nor by what means they got them, they are apt to reverence them as sacred things, and not to suffer them to be profaned, touched, or questioned. They look on them as the *Urim*

and *Thummim* set up in their minds immediately by God Himself, to be the great and unerring deciders of truth and falsehood, and the judges to which they are to appeal in all manner of controversies. (*ECHU* 4.20.9, emphasis added)

No doubt this is why the law of fashion has no common name, since it is everywhere assumed to be divine law.[12]

These variable religious beliefs outside the law of nature stand out in their potential irrationality, even in people who are otherwise reasonable. These beliefs act as "internal oracles" overruling propositions "how clearly soever proved": "Men will disbelieve their own eyes, renounce the evidence of their senses, and give their own experience the lie, rather than admit anything disagreeing with these sacred tenets" (*ECHU* 4.20.10). Opinion ingrained by custom, however absurd, is even capable of overpowering the natural desire for preservation.

[T]here are great numbers of opinions, which, by men of different countries, educations, and tempers, are received and embraced as first and unquestionable principles; many whereof, both for their absurdity, as well as oppositions one to another, it is impossible should be true. But yet all those propositions, how remote soever from reason, are so sacred somewhere or other, that men even of good understanding in other matters, will sooner part with their lives and whatever is dearest to them, than suffer themselves to doubt, or others to question, the truth of them. (*ECHU* 1.3.21)

For this reason, Locke calls custom "a greater power than nature" (*ECHU* 1.3.25). When we consider the role of what, in the *Second Treatise*, he calls "fundamental, sacred, unalterable law of self-preservation" for the law of nature, we see that the variable part of the law of fashion can overpower the part that coincides with natural law and thereby override the very reason "for which [men]

---

[12] Cf. *Questions,* 127, 149.

entered into society" (*2T* 149).[13]

The part of the law of fashion that is of greatest concern to Locke thus poses a fundamental problem for the prospect of directing political society to its proper end as determined by reason and the law of nature. And, to repeat, the problem is not limited to those one would most obviously associate with fanaticism, but is pervasive in those who are generally reasonable. In the final chapter of Book 2 of the *Essay*,[14] Locke asks why it is that what seems self-evidently true to one seems absurd to another. How can two persons who regard one another as otherwise sensible seem to each other, with regard to certain opinions, astonishingly obstinate? Self-love, Locke says, does not fully account for it. "Prejudice is a generally good name" for the phenomenon, but it "reaches not the bottom of the disease," which is a "sort of madness" that springs up in otherwise "very sober and rational minds" (*ECHU* 2.33.3). The root cause of this "disease" is the "connection of ideas wholly owing to chance or custom, ideas that in themselves are not all of kin, [but] come to be so united in men's minds that it is very hard to separate them," such that "the one no sooner at any time comes into the understanding but its associate appears with it, and if there are more than two which are thus united, the whole gang always inseparable

---

[13] "And thus, men do not feel themselves bound by that law, which nature seems to have fixed even in the souls of brutes, and they surpass wild beasts in their savagery. Yet if there exists a law of nature, which might appear to be the most sacred among men, which the entire human race seems driven to obey by a certain natural instinct and its own interests, this is surely that of self-preservation, which some establish for this reason as the primary and fundamental law of nature. But, such is the power of custom and opinion, which is not innate but derives from some external source, adopted from the conduct of daily life that it arms men even against themselves, and brings them to lay violent hands upon themselves and pursue death with the same eagerness with which others flee from it" (*Questions*, p. 191). Cf. *2T* 11, 17, 19, 25, 123, 128, 129, 135.

[14] The title of the chapter ("Of the Association of Ideas") recalls the title of the chapter on moral relations and the law of fashion ("Of other relations," i.e. relations of ideas).

show themselves together" (*ECHU* 2.33.5). Thus "custom settles habits of thinking in the understanding" (*ECHU* 2.33.6). These "intellectual habits…work as strongly, and produce as regular effects as if they were natural, and are therefore called so" (*ECHU* 2.33.7). Such habits can ingrain even crude superstition for a lifetime (*ECHU* 2.33.10). And "[s]ome such wrong and unnatural combinations of ideas will be found to establish the irreconcilable opposition between different sects of philosophy and religion" (*ECHU* 2.33.18). We can now see the connection between the law of fashion and the most central concerns of Locke's political enterprise.

But if Locke offers a more precise diagnosis of the disease, his diagnosis of those inextricably riveted ideas may cause despair of a cure. In *Of the Conduct of the Understanding* he acknowledges that in the *Essay*, he had not sought to "to enquire into the remedies [that] ought to be applied to…[the] unnatural connections [that] become by custom as natural to the mind as sun and light," a state that "is as frequent a cause of mistake and error in us as perhaps anything else that can be named, and is a disease of the mind as hard to be cured as any" (*CU* 41). The cure lies, at least in part, in developing the "vigor of mind able to contest the empire of habit and look into its own principles." But this is "a freedom which few men have the notion of in themselves, and fewer are allowed the practice of by others," and so Locke looks to rebuild from the ground up through *education*: "the common and most general miscarriages which I think men should avoid or rectify in a right conduct of their understandings…should be particularly taken care of in education" (*CU* 12).[15]

In the first place, this means avoiding the formation of the problematic intellectual habits in question: "I can see no other right way of principling [children], but to take heed, as much as may be,

---

[15] Cf. Aristotle, *Politics*, tr. Carnes Lord (Chicago: University of Chicago Press, 1984) 1337a12–14: "That the legislator must, therefore, make the education of the young his object above all would be disputed by no one."

that in their tender years ideas that have no natural cohesion come not to be united in their heads" (*CU* 41). By avoiding exposure to the association of ideas not naturally related, a sound education will avoid as much as possible instilling the root cause of sectarian strife. Accordingly, in *Some Thoughts Concerning Education*, the recommended theological education of children will be minimal. From an early age, a child ought to have "imprinted on his mind a true notion of God, as of the independent Supreme Being, Author and Maker of all things, from whom we receive all our good, who loves us and gives us all things" (*STCE* 136). But parents should be wary of saying much more about God for fear that a child's head will "be either filled with false or perplexed with unintelligible notions of [God]," leading him either to superstition or atheism. Even the notion that God "sees and hears everything and does all manner of good to those that love and obey him" should be mentioned "only upon occasion" (*STCE* 136). Children should not be permitted to read indiscriminately from the Bible, but only select Old Testament stories and "easy and plain moral rules" (*STCE* 159). Perhaps nothing worse could be found for children to read than the Bible in its entirety, or indiscriminately, which would likely lead to an "odd jumble of thoughts" at a "tender age": "I am apt to think that this in some men has been the very reason why they never had clear and distinct thoughts of it all their lifetime" (*STCE* 158).

Avoidance, however, is not enough "to contest the empire of habit" in the mind. Habit *per se* is not the problem, and indeed habit has a fundamental role to play in Lockean education: "The business [of education] in respect of knowledge is not, as I think, to perfect a learner in all or any one of the sciences, but to give his mind that freedom, that disposition, and those habits that may enable him to attain any part of knowledge he shall apply himself to, or stand in need of, in the future course of his life" (*CU* 12). Most basically, the habituated capacity to resist present pleasures and pains is the underpinning of Locke's educational program and is the "true foundation of future ability and happiness" (*STCE* 45).[16] Moreover, Locke discourages parents and educators from imposing rules on children when they can instill habits instead. Rules can be forgotten or ignored, whereas habit makes behaviors "easy and natural" (*STCE* 66). Habit is particularly useful for instilling the "great social virtue" of justice in children (and not only children), who are "guided more by self-love than reason or reflection" and are thus "apt to deviate from the just measures of right and wrong." For "habits work[] more constantly and with greater facility than reason, which when we have most need of it is seldom fairly consulted, and more rarely obeyed" (*STCE* 110).[17]

It would be a mistake, however, to suppose that Locke simply saw habit as an alternative to reason, or even as a disciplinary preparation for a mature rationality that would supplant habit. Habit is essential to the formation and operation of the mind; it "makes the mind what it is," for better or worse (*CU* 4). Not only are the defects of the mind frequently misattributed to nature rather than habit, but so too are its "excellences." The difference in natural intellectual capacity is far less than is supposed by those who neglect the formative role of habit. Indeed, the greatest part of our knowledge, Locke says in the *Essay*, is "habitual knowledge."[18] It is difficult indeed to ex-

---

[16] Cf. Rita Koganzon, "'Contesting the Empire of Habit': Habituation and Liberty in Lockean Education," *American Political Science Review*, 110 (2016): 547–58.

[17] Cf. Aristotle, *Nicomachean Ethics*, tr. Robert C. Bartlett and Susan D. Collins (Chicago: University of Chicago Press). "[M]oral virtue is the result of habit…It makes no small difference, then, whether one is habituated in this or that way straight from childhood but a very great difference—or rather the whole difference" (1103a16, 1103b23–25).

[18] All knowledge that is not currently in "the present view of the mind" (which Locke calls "actual knowledge") is "so lodged…in [one's] memory that whenever that proposition comes again to be reflected on, he, without doubt of hesitation embraces the right side, assents to it, and is certain of the truth in it…this, I think, one may call habitual knowledge." Without habitual knowledge, "[men] would be all very ignorant, [a]nd he that knew most would know but one truth, that being all he was able to think on at one time" (*ECHU* 4.1.8).

amine critically one's own intellectual habits so as to distinguish ideas or associations that are unwarranted but seem obvious through habituation from those that are "habitual knowledge." Nevertheless, being alert to the potential defects present in the understanding through intellectual habit can itself be made an intellectual habit. The proper "principling" of children requires "that this rule be often inculcated to them to be their guide in the whole course of their lives and studies, viz. that they never suffer any ideas to be joined in their understandings in any other or stronger combination than what their own nature and correspondence give them; and that they often examine those that they find linked together in their minds, whether this association of ideas be from the visible agreement that is in the ideas themselves, or from the habitual and prevailing custom of the mind joining them thus together in thinking" (*CU* 41). Children should be trained in the "rule" of critically examining the association of their ideas, with a view to expunging those that are present owing *merely* to "habitual and prevailing custom." By speaking of inculcating a rule, Locke implies that contesting the empire of habit entails instilling new habits, which, as Rita Koganzon puts it, "are actually counterhabits intended to preempt those habits which...fashion would otherwise instill."[19]

And yet, as Locke makes clear in his account of habit in the *Conduct of the Understanding*, habituation of a child's mind is frequently directed and encouraged by praise, which is to say, by opinion, reputation, and therefore fashion (*CU* 4). The counterhabits of Lockean education are not meant simply to pre-empt habits that fashion would instill; they are to be directed and encouraged by a *new fashion*. The power of reputation is no less fundamental to Lockean education than the power of habit. Indeed, reputation is "the great secret of education" (*CU* 56). The importance of reputation in education returns us to the vital importance of punishment and reward for directing human behavior, a point he reiterates in *Some Thoughts Concerning Education*: "Good and evil, reward and punishment, are the only motives to a rational creature" (*STCE* 53).

---

[19] Koganz0n 2016, 548

And from what we have seen in the *Essay*, we should not be surprised that Locke would recommend employing the most effective sort of reward and punishment:

> The rewards and punishments...whereby we should keep children in order are...of that force that when we can get them once to work, the business, I think, is done and the difficulty is over. Esteem and disgrace are, of all others, the most powerful incentives to the mind, when once it is brought to relish them. If you can once get into children the love of credit and an apprehension of shame and disgrace, you have put into them the true principle, which will constantly incline them to the right. (*STCE* 56)[20]

Not only does Locke employ the law of fashion, he seeks to *strengthen* it. He would see "the sense of esteem and disgrace sink the deeper and be the more of weight" by bringing children to believe that what brings them esteem at home will be "beloved and cherished by everybody" and will, moreover, allow them to enjoy "all other good things as a consequence"; whereas what leads to disgrace at home will cause them to fall into "neglect and contempt, and in that state the want of whatever might satisfy or delight [them] will follow" (*STCE* 58). It is thus imperative to be mindful of the "company they converse with and the fashion of those around them" (*STCE* 67). With their sensitivity to reputation thus heightened, "you may turn them as you please, and they will be in love with all the ways of virtue" (*STCE* 58). Locke admits that reputation is "not the true principle and measure of virtue...yet it is that which comes nearest to it...and is the proper guide and encouragement of chil-

---

[20] Cf. Aristotle, *Nicomachean Ethics*: "speeches appear to have the capacity to exhort and to incite those youths who are free/liberal, and to make someone who has a wellborn character and is truly a lover of what is noble receptive to virtue. Yet speeches are incapable of exhorting the many to nobility and gentlemanliness. For the many are not naturally obedient to the governance supplied by a sense of shame but rather to that supplied by fear..." (1179b7–12). "For some things one even ought to fear, and it is noble and shameful not to—for example, disrepute..." (1115a13).

dren, till they grow able to judge themselves and to find what is right by their own reason" (*STCE* 61).

Locke thus appears to imply that the law of reputation in children is intended to give way to the law of nature. And yet, although Locke's moral education is presumably intended to direct children to the law of nature, his educational program includes no attempt to instruct in the rational discovery of its content, except for suggesting their reading Cicero's *De Officiis* when old enough to do so (*STCE* 185, cf. *RC* 241–243). Even then, Locke blurs the line between reason and fashion by suggesting that the "knowledge of virtue" has been provided "all along from the beginning, in all the instances [the child] is capable of, being taught him more by practice than rules; and the love of reputation instead of satisfying his appetite being made habitual in him" (*STCE* 185). Thus, as Michelle Brady points out, moral enforcement is left overwhelmingly to reputation. Noting how minimal the education in theology will be, Brady observes that "reference to an eternal reward is always kept implicit...and the idea of eternal punishment is surprisingly absent...The reward and punishment children actually see, on the basis of which they make their choices, is always a matter of esteem and shame."[21]

---

[21] Michelle Brady, "Locke's Thoughts on Reputation," *Review of Politics*, 75 (2013): 349. Cf. the opening pages of the *Reasonableness of Christianity*, where Locke interprets Scripture as teaching that the unsaved are deprived of eternal life and sentenced to death, which does not mean "endless torment in hell-fire," but instead "a ceasing to be" (*RC* 2–4). Cf. also *ECHU* 1.3.13: "...it being impossible that men should without shame or fear confidently and serenely break a rule which they could not but evidently know that God had set up and would certainly punish the breach of...to a degree to make it a very ill bargain for the transgressor. Without such knowledge as this, a man can never be certain that any thing is his duty. Ignorance or doubt of the law, hopes to escape the knowledge or power of the law-maker, or the like, may make men give way to a present appetite: but let anyone see the fault and the rod by it and with the transgression a fire ready to punish; a pleasure tempting and the hand of the Almighty visibly held up and prepared to take vengeance...and then tell me whether it be possible for people with such a prospect as this, wantonly,

And since "reward and punishment are the only motives to a rational creature" (*STCE* 53), Locke provides "a much firmer [rational basis for the law of fashion] than he provides for obeying natural law."[22] Indeed, although in the course of discussing civil law he makes reference to "the natural rights of men, and the origins and foundations of society and the duties resulting from thence" to be learned from reading Pufendorf and Grotius (*STCE* 186), nowhere in his book on education does he refer to natural law. It is true that Lockean education espouses "the right improvement and exercise of our reason" as "the highest perfection that a man can attain to in this life" and which therefore "deserves the greatest care and attention in cultivating it" (*STCE* 122). But whether the right exercise of reason entails natural law is unclear.[23]

Whatever the case may be, Locke recognizes that "learners must first be believers" (*CU* 34). Initially, at least, moral principles can be instilled only through the same means as any custom: reputation and habit. But, as Ruth Grant points out, the custom of Lockean education is of a novel sort, being a custom that disdains custom in the name of independent reasoning for oneself. Like all custom, it operates through praise and blame, its own law of fashion, as can be seen in Locke's flattery of parents who follow his educational program as being "so irregularly bold that they dare venture to consult their own reason in the education of their children rather than rely wholly upon old custom" (*STCE* 216). We may call the new custom, following Grant, a "reasonable custom," provided we distinguish the reasonable from the genuinely rational.[24]

---

and without scruple, to offend against a law..."; and *ECHU* 2.20.14: "Pleasure operates not so strongly on us as pain"; Owen 2015, 85–86.

[22] Brady 2013, 348.

[23] *Of the Conduct of the Understanding* likewise makes no mention of natural law, although cf. 44.

[24] Ruth Grant, "Locke on Custom's Power and Reason's Authority," *Review of Politics*, 74 (2012): 621. On the distinction between reasonableness and rationality in Locke, cf. Joseph Carrig, "Liberal Impediments to Liberal Education: The Assent to Locke," *Review of Politics*, 63 (2001): 61–63; Thomas L. Pangle, The Spirit of Modern Republicanism (Chicago:

Doubtless, Locke must have supposed that the new model of education would provide an easier and wider pathway to genuine rationality and independence of thought, by both shedding the most absurd irrationalities and by using esteem and disgrace to direct young minds away from authoritative custom and toward authoritative reason. But just how easy and wide could Locke have expected the path to genuine rationality blazed by the new education to be? Yes, "learners must first be believers," but it is also true that children receive notions "riveted [into the mind] by long custom and education beyond all possibility of being pulled out again" (*ECHU* 4.20.9). It is not only learners who must be believers, but, as Locke says in the *Reasonableness of Christianity*, "the greatest part [of mankind] cannot know, and therefore they must believe" (*RC* 243). Can the new custom possibly be limited to education? Or must it not be part of what Grant calls a broader "project of cultural reform"?[25] Must Locke not expect that the greatest part of mankind will continue to be governed "chiefly, if not solely" by the law of fashion (*ECHU* 2.28.12)? And might not this insight provide a key to Locke's broader strategy? For fashion is more powerful than government, or even religion. Or, government and religion derive their power primarily from fashion. And so, as Locke says in the journal entry cited at the outset: "[h]e...that would govern the world well, had need consider rather what fashions he makes, than what [civil] laws; and to bring anything into use he need only give it reputation."[26]

At this point, we must recall that the law of fashion is twofold: the part that coincides with the law of nature and is more or less the same everywhere, and the part that varies. The former part, even though it is embraced through fashion rather than reason, is never the object of his attack. The latter part, however, becomes

---

University of Chicago Press), 264–265; Steven Forde, "What Does Locke Expect Us to Know?" *Review of Politics*, 68 (2006): 255–258; Owen 2015, 89.

[25] Grant 2012, 621.

[26] https://blog.umd.edu/slaverylawandpower/john-locke-an-essay-on-reputation/

associated with a disease of the mind, "a sort of madness" (*ECHU* 2.33.3), requiring a penetrating analysis to diagnose and a radical educational and cultural reform to cure. This disease of the mind leads to irreconcilable opposition not only between societies but, more destructively, between sects. We can thus think about Locke's project of cultural reform as being, at least in part, a reform of the part of the law of fashion that heretofore has varied and conflicted. The beachhead of his reform, then, would be religious reform; and the new reasonable custom would somehow entail "the reasonableness of Christianity." Christianity cannot be reduced to "pure natural religion" (*RC* 1). It must include revelation and point the way to salvation. But its revealed truth will serve chiefly to instruct "the illiterate bulk of mankind" in the points "most necessary" for their salvation; i.e. in their most necessary moral duties. These are not the moral rules that differ by country and sect, but those indicated by the law of nature. Christian revelation thus confirms and does not extend beyond the law of nature, except insofar as revelation is necessary to do what reason has thus far been unable to do, viz. to place those moral rules on their true foundation as commands of a God with the power to enforce them (*RC* 241–242). The substantive demands of a reasonable Christianity would thus coincide as far as possible with the "several moral rules" of the law of nature, which "receive from mankind a very general approbation" and which "men, without renouncing all sense and reason, and their own interests, which they are so constantly true to, could not generally mistake" (*ECHU* 1.3.6, 2.28.11). Meanwhile, the new Christianity will declare every controversial matter of faith—the opinions that divide the sects—as "indifferent." It will mock the idea of orthodoxy ("every church is orthodox to itself"), while declaring the "mark of the true church" to be nothing related to any such controversy, but rather toleration, as preservation requires.[27] Just as the new custom disdains custom, so toleration will be the new orthodoxy that dis-

---

[27] Locke, *A Letter Concerning Toleration*, tr. William Popple (Indianapolis: Hackett), 23.

dains orthodoxy.[28] The new law of fashion will thus be shorn as much as possible of the part that extends beyond the law of nature, the part that admits of irreconcilable variation. If, however, the ineffective law of nature in fact becomes subsumed by the most effective law of fashion, it is not altogether clear that divine law, natural or other, retains a function.[29]

Although the law of fashion does not feature in Locke's political works proper, its having been tucked away in the middle of the *Essay Concerning Human Understanding* does not diminish its enormous importance for Locke's broader teaching, including not least his political teaching. Once we are attuned to its importance, we are left with many questions that require a reassessment of familiar aspects of that teaching.

Why, for example, does Locke make no mention of the law of fashion in the *Second Treatise*, if throughout history most of mankind have governed themselves by it? What becomes of the famous doctrine of the origins of political society in an "original compact" between individuals who are "by nature, all free, equal and independent" (*2T* 95)? Why does Locke say that the first established, settled, known law is civil law, made by whatever form of commonwealth the majority of individuals party to the original compact determine (*2T* 124, 132, 134)? It seems difficult, to say the least, to square the great historical prevalence of the law of fashion with what would appear to be the core teaching of the *Second Treatise*. It is true that Locke offers a less prominent alternative account of "the original of common-wealths," according to which we find "in the first ages of the world" small patriarchies in which it was "easy and almost natural for children by tacit and scarce avoidable consent to make way for the father's authority and government," allowing "the

---

[28] Cf. Owen 2015, 62–67. On "indifferency" in relation to custom, orthodoxy, and zealous bigotry, cf. *CU* 34.

[29] Cf. Forde 2006, 258, Strauss 1953, 211–214, Owen 2015, 97–102, 107–112. Cf. also *ECHU* 1.4.8, end.

father of the family to become the Prince of it" (*2T* 105, 74–75). From here alliances formed with neighboring families where, in an age of "innocence and sincerity," the "*custom* of obeying [the father] in their childhood made it easier to submit" to the most pre-eminent man as "a kind of natural authority," which "by a tacit consent devolved into his hands" (*2T* 94, 105; cf. 107, emphasis added). Which, then, is the true account of the origins of political society— the original compact to exit the state of nature or the tacit consent supported by the custom of paternal authority? The latter is not only more historically plausible, but, with one of the few references to custom in the *Second Treatise*, it has the advantage of being far easier to reconcile with his statements on the law of fashion. Is the story of the original compact in the state of nature, agreed to by express not tacit consent, then, a fiction—a sort of founding myth of the new rationalistic custom, intended to elicit tacit consent and transform tacit consent into express consent?

As we grow to appreciate the importance of the new custom and its law of fashion for Locke's writings as a whole, we are furthermore forced to wonder what becomes of genuine rationality. For a prejudice in favor of reason remains a prejudice. There is, to be sure, a *prima facie* plausibility to the notion that a prejudice in favor of reason, when combined with the removal of the most absurd irrationalities, will offer the smoothest and broadest path to genuine rationality, particularly if the habit of critical examination of ideas, in a search for those that are present by mere habit and custom, alerts one to their operation even in the case of the most reasonable custom. Genuine rationality, then, requires a critical examination of the liberal law of fashion, an examination to which the liberal law of fashion points but which it cannot survive as such. On the other hand, it is also plausible that the new fashion will flatter those formed by it into supposing that they are already in fact free thinkers because they praise free thinking and sneer at custom.[30] Might the new prejudice be harder to detect as such? Moreover, mustn't

---

[30] Cf. Nathan Tarcov, *Locke's Education for Liberty*, (Chicago: University of Chicago Press, 1984), 94; Brady 2013, 356.

the "customs" at which fashionable free thinkers sneer be taken seriously as what they purport to be, which is not mere custom in the most important cases? Is there not far more at stake in religious disagreement than what Locke's notions of "custom" and especially "fashion" can capture?

What, by Locke's account, ultimately is the difference between the way of life of a rational human being and that of a merely reasonable one? Locke's own life would attest that the truly rational human being is about more than peaceable toleration, preservation, industriousness, and accumulation of property.[31] Yet Locke almost seems intent to discourage the purely theoretical investigations that he himself pursued with such exacting determination (*ECHU* 4.3.22, 25). His educational program declares natural philosophy a failed enterprise with no future (*STCE* 190). We note that music is dropped from the education of children as a particularly useless variety of recreation (*STCE* 197). Aristotle, in contrast, made music the centerpiece of the education of children in part because precisely its lack of utility marked it as an activity of *leisure*, which, as opposed to recreation and work, was the category of activity that at its peak in philosophy promised happiness.[32] As Locke presents it, even happiness is not so appealing, consisting chiefly in the alleviation of chronic uneasiness, which varies according to our tastes. Study and knowledge are no surer means to happiness than hawking and hunting, or even luxury and debauchery (*ECHU* 2.21.54). There is no greatest good in life, which is occupied with an endless *pursuit* of happiness.[33] That pursuit is driven more by avoidance of pains than enjoyment of fleeting pleasures, which are in any case a matter of taste (*ECHU* 2.21.43-44, 55). Now that we are, in fact, many gen-

---

[31] Cf. Locke's epitaph: "If you ask what kind of a man he was, he answers that he lived content with his own small fortune. Bred a scholar, he made his learning subservient only to the cause of truth."

[32] *Politics* 1337b27–1338b4, cf. *Nicomachean Ethics* 1177b4 and context, 1144a4–5.

[33] Cf. Strauss 1953, 249-251; Aristotle, *Nicomachean Ethics* 1177a23–28; Plato, *The Republic*, tr. Allan Bloom (New York: Basic Books, 1968) 519b7–c7.

erations into the massive cultural transformation launched by Locke and kindred spirits, we have a right to wonder why, despite the evident success of that transformation in many respects, rationalism has lost appeal and fallen out of fashion, even, if not precisely, among liberals.[34]

---

[34] Cf. J. Judd Owen, *Religion and the Demise of Liberal Rationalism* (Chicago: University of Chicago Press, 2001), 1–4, 170–171.

5

WHY NOT UNIVERSAL HOME-SCHOOLING? JOHN LOCKE AND THE LIBERAL OBJECTION TO INSTITUTIONAL EDUCATION

Rita Koganzon

Why Not Homeschooling?

Before the coronavirus pandemic closed nearly all American schools in 2020, the idea of mass homeschooling in the United States was basically unimaginable. The percentage of American children being homeschooled never went above four percent before that, and even those few families who did it were held in suspicion by the professional educational establishment and large portions of the public.[1] Professional educators fear that homeschooling is just cover for extreme religious and ideological indoctrination, if not outright abuse.[2] The public, while willing to tolerate the practice as a matter of parental right, still viewed homeschoolers as likely to become so-

---

[1] "Number and percentage of homeschooled students ages 5 through 17 with a grade equivalent of kindergarten through 12th grade," Digest of Educational Statistics, US Department of Education, 2018. https://nces.ed.gov/programs/digest/d18/tables/dt18_206.10.asp.

[2] This is an old view recently given new life by Tara Westover's popular memoir of her abusive homeschooling experience, *Educated: A Memoir* (Random House, 2018). See, e.g., Elizabeth Bartholet, "Homeschooling: Parent Rights Absolutism vs. Child Rights to Education & Protection," *Arizona Law Review* 62 (2020); James Dwyer and Shawn Peters, *Homeschooling: The History and Philosophy of a Controversial Practice* (Chicago: University of Chicago Press, 2019).

cially maladjusted.[3] But by April 2020, all these misgivings gave way to the urgency of a public health crisis, and within a matter of weeks, almost every family in the country was homeschooling.

To say Americans were happy about this development would be an overstatement. While some children and parents welcomed the reprieve from the social and time pressures of school, work commutes, and regimented schedules, there was little time to prepare and the conditions were not ideal. Parents still had to work, or they suddenly found themselves out of work and had to do something about that, and everyone had to adjust to a radically changed daily life under quarantine. Teaching their children was not easily integrated into these demands.

Although the pandemic is an exceptional case, it illustrates quite clearly why the US was never very hospitable to mass homeschooling. Even at the Founding, long before the state capacity to build it existed, Americans promoted not just schooling, but comprehensive *systems* of public schools. In 1779, Thomas Jefferson proposed a state-wide system of local grammar schools that would identify the state's best students and channel them into district secondary schools, which would in turn send the best of their students to a state university.[4] Benjamin Rush expanded Jefferson's ambitions to the national stage, and published a plan whereby "the whole state will be tied together by one system of education" that would "convert men into republican machines."[5] The American Philosophical Society offered a prize in 1795 for the best "essay on a system of liberal education, and literary instruction, adapted to the genius of the government, and best calculated to promote the general welfare of the United States." The submissions, which have become canonical works of early American educational thinking, all followed the

---

[3] Richard Medlin, "Home schooling and the question of socialization," *Peabody Journal of Education* 75 (2000): 107–123.

[4] Thomas Jefferson, "A Bill for the More General Diffusion of Knowledge," 18 June 1779.

[5] Benjamin Rush, "Thoughts Upon the Mode of Education Proper in a Republic," *Essays on Education in the Early Republic*, ed. Frederick Rudolph (Cambridge: Belknap Press, 1965).

Society's presumption that American education would be national and institutional.[6] Indeed, nearly all the major educational writings of the early republican period proposed universal and cheap or free public schooling.[7]

Most writers of the Founding period assumed that parents would be eager to send children to public schools, if only such schools could be brought into existence. And they were right—the eventual nationwide triumph of the common school movement in the nineteenth century was largely due to widespread parental desire for it rather than any coercive pressure exerted by the state.[8] This is because the greatest advantage of public schools was their promised cost savings. The Delaware schoolteacher Robert Coram argued that a single system of public schools would be cheaper to maintain than many independently-administered private academies, and Samuel Harrison Smith pointed out that the cost of home education was prohibitive for most Americans: "If parents educate their children, the hours withdrawn from business would impoverish them."[9]

And this is the key point. Public schooling in America was desirable because it was necessary. America was even then the "all middle class" nation, as John Stuart Mill described in his review of *Democracy in America*, where the vast majority of people had to work—on the farm, in the home, and in the skilled trades—for their living (and, in many cases, that work required their children's help)

---

[6] Benjamin Justice, "'The Great Contest': The American Philosophical Society Education Prize of 1795 and the Problem of American Education," *American Journal of Education* 114 (2008): 191–213.

[7] Rita Koganzon, "'Producing a Reconciliation of Disinterestedness and Commerce': The Political Rhetoric of Education in the Early Republic," *History of Education Quarterly* 52 (2012): 403–429.

[8] David Tyack, *The One Best System* (Cambridge: Harvard University Press, 1974), 66–69.

[9] Robert Coram, "Political inquiries: to which is added, a plan for the general establishment of schools throughout the United States" (Wilmington, DE: 1791); Samuel Harrison Smith, *Remarks on Education, Illustrating the Close Connection Between Wisdom and Virtue* (Philadelphia: John Omrod, 1797), 66.

and, beyond teaching them reading and writing at home in the winters, devoting themselves to giving their children a complete education was simply impossible.

Locke's Case Against Schools

The democratic necessity of schools for an all-middle class society did not, however, imply an equal philosophical necessity. Indeed, although Americans could draw on a long republican tradition favoring public schooling, a liberal counter-argument had more recently begun to coalesce in the influential works of John Locke, Jean-Jacques Rousseau, and later Adam Smith and J. S. Mill, that called into question the benefits of schooling for individual freedom.

Locke's *Some Thoughts Concerning Education*, published in 1693, was one of the first works to advance a *liberal* argument against schooling, grounded in the epistemology of his *Essay Concerning Human Understanding* and his account of liberty in the *Two Treatises of Government*. The freedom he emphasized was individual freedom—from intellectual domination by custom, fashion, and prejudice—rather than the collective freedom of the republic.[10] A strong republic requires uniformity in belief and conduct, but the cultivation of such uniformity through education threatens intellectual freedom. Schools, with their standardized curricula and social rule of children, threatened the freedom that Locke wanted education to foster, so he argued that education should take place in the home, under the guidance of tutors or, better yet, parents.

In the *Essay*, Locke offers a pessimistic account of the possibilities for intellectual liberty. The most powerful determinant of our

---

[10] A more thorough account of Locke's view of intellectual freedom than I can give here is in Rita Koganzon, "'Contesting the Empire of Habit': Habituation and Liberty in Lockean Education," *American Political Science Review* 110 (2016): 547–558. This article, as well as my book, *Liberal States, Authoritarian Families: Childhood and Education in Early Modern Thought* (New York: Oxford, 2021), elaborate several points in this section and extend them to issues in Locke's philosophy that go beyond his encouragement of home education.

actions and beliefs, he argues, is not the positive law legislated by governments or even the divine law enjoined on us by religion, nor by any means is it reason. Rather, it is what he calls the "law of fashion": "The greatest part govern themselves chiefly, if not solely, by this Law of Fashion; and so they do that, which keeps them in Reputation with their Company, little regard the Laws of God, or the Magistrate" (*ECHU* 2.28.12).[11] Not only do men govern themselves with this law, but they corrupt themselves with it: "Fashion and the common opinion having settled wrong notions, and education and custom ill habits, the just values of things are misplaced, and the palates of men corrupted" (*ECHU* 2.21.69). Most of life's activity is driven by "fantastical uneasiness, (as itch after honour, power, or riches, etc.) which acquir'd habits by fashion, example, and education have setled in us, and a thousand other irregular desires, which custom has made natural to us" (ECHU 2.21.44–45). All our activity is in pursuit of some desire, but only a few of our desires arise from natural necessities like hunger and cold. The vast majority of our mature desires are "fantastical" ones, acquired in the course of our upbringing and education, from the amorphous forces of custom and fashion.

We might hope for a government that can keep the law of fashion in check, managing public opinion so that it is oriented towards virtue. But unlike positive or even divine law, the law of fashion has neither legislator nor executor; it is self-generating and self-enforcing. No one can reliably direct it, and all political efforts to manage and channel it will have unpredictable and, at best, partial results. "The law of opinion or reputation" is a shadow government; it "establishes itself in the several societies, tribes, and clubs of men in the world...by a secret and tacit consent" (*ECHU* 2.28.10–12). There is no point in hoping that good laws or good government can save us from corrupt public opinion. The very structure of the

---

[11] All citations from the *Essay* here are by book, chapter and section number, and come from the Clarendon edition: John Locke, *Essay Concerning Human Understanding*, ed. Peter Nidditch (Oxford: Clarendon Press, 1975).

Lockean state—with its representative government and legislative supremacy—only increases the influence of public opinion. Our best hope for freedom lies in ourselves. We can try to understand the structure and tendencies of our own minds, and their susceptibility to fashion's power, and to discipline ourselves against it. Teaching us how to do this, in large part, is the purpose of Locke's brief mental training manual for adults, *On the Conduct of the Understanding*.

But since so much of fashion's power over us takes root in childhood, education is an especially sensitive undertaking for those who hope to form individuals capable of intellectual freedom. "Custom settles habits of Thinking in the Understanding, as well as of Determining in the Will...which once set a going continue on in the same steps they have been used to" (*ECHU* 2.33.6). If it is the case that men mainly "do that, which keeps them in Reputation with their Company," then it becomes imperative to ensure that their first company is virtuous company. Given both the premium that Locke puts on reasonableness and the ubiquity of the obstacles he sees to achieving it, the urgency of keeping children away from pernicious influences motivates his turn to home education.

Children act as much in pursuit of desires as everyone else, and their strongest desire is for "esteem." "Esteem and disgrace are, of all others, the most powerful incentives to the mind...which I look on as the great secret of education" (*STCE* 56).[12] Esteem is the impetus for imitation and is thus the most educative of desires. But esteem must come *from* someone, and whoever becomes the arbiter of esteem and disgrace for a child takes on an enormous authority over him. The danger is that nearly anyone can exercise such authority over a child simply by dispensing esteem and disgrace, so Locke warns repeatedly of "the great danger from...servants, and other ill-ordered children" (*STCE* 19, 59, 68–70, 76, 89, 107, 138). Their authority is either irresponsible or malicious: servants are not held to

---

[12] Citations from *Some Thoughts* is by section from the following edition: John Locke, *Some Thoughts Concerning Education* and *On the Conduct of the Understanding*, eds. Nathan Tarcov and Ruth Grant (Indianapolis: Hackett, 1996).

account for the way children turn out, nor do they have a strong self-interest in a good outcome. Fellow children are even worse authorities, since they exploit each other's desire to be liked, creating arbitrary and even morally pernicious social hierarchies to subordinate and compel conformity.

Children's social worlds exemplify on a small scale the tyrannical potential of the law of fashion—their rules are arbitrary and constantly changing, but enforced with unrelenting zeal. As children habitually angle to remain in the favor of their classmates, they lose the habits of mind that permit intellectual liberty. Left to their own devices with other children, the child's ideas and values are derived from "the prevailing infection of his fellows" (*STCE* 70). Consequently, Locke warns parents against schools because the sheer preponderance of the young in them undermines adult authority and replaces it with the tyranny of other boys:

> Till you can find a school, wherein it is possible for the master to look after the manners of his scholars, and can show as great effects of his care of forming their minds to virtue, and their carriage to good breeding, as of forming their tongues to the learned languages; you must confess, that you...think it worth while to hazard your son's innocence and virtue, for a little Greek and Latin...He that considers how diametrically opposite the skill of living well, and managing, as a man should do, his affairs in the world, is to that malapertness, tricking, or violence, learnt among school-boys, will think the faults of a privater education infinitely to be preferred to such improvements; and will take care to preserve his child's innocence and modesty at home, as being nearer of kin, and more in the way of those qualities, which make a useful and able man. (*STCE* 70)

The most straightforward shortcoming of schools is that even potentially salutary adult authorities in them are always vastly outnumbered by children. "Let the master's industry and skill be ever so great," Locke warns, "it is impossible he should have 50 or 100 scholars under his eye...the forming of their minds and manners requiring a constant attention, and particular application to every single boy; which is impossible in a numerous flock" (*STCE* 70).

Parents at home, by contrast, can attend more carefully to their much smaller flock. They can individuate education, and, more importantly, they can stand between children to pre-empt that tyranny over one another that develops where adult authority is outnumbered. They also stand between children and the broader world to delay and diminish the even more powerful pull that its fashions will have on them. To achieve this, authority has to be exclusive to parents and extended at their discretion to the few others they deem acceptable influences, so that the moral influence that authority exerts is in the first place consistent, but perhaps even more importantly, so that it is purposeful and understands itself as such.

Locke flatters parents by presuming that they are better suited to rule their own children than anyone else is, commending his readers for being "so irregularly bold, that they dare venture to consult their own reason, in the education of their children, rather than wholly to rely upon old custom" (*STCE* 216). But this is not because he thinks that his readers necessarily *are* more reasonable than their servants or the neighborhood children, or less susceptible to the corruption of popular opinion. Even conscientious parents are prone to error and most are unlikely to start out conscientious, but the long duration of the relationship between parents and children offers an inducement to parents to consider the long-term effects of their decisions more carefully. Their children will inherit not just their property but their personal legacies. There is simply far more at stake for parents in childrearing than for anyone else who deals with their children.

Moreover, the *process* of Lockean childrearing works to improve parents' morals. For parents to establish their authority as dispensers of esteem and disgrace, their children must be induced to fall "in love with the company of their parents," but this requires that parents make themselves lovable, mainly by spending a great deal of time with them (*STCE* 70). In order to direct their children's wills, they must first "will for them," and as they grow, parents must serve as constant confidants and advisors, fearing nothing more than that their children should desire to confide in anyone *but* them. Everything in Locke's pedagogy, from his prohibition against swaddling, which immobilized infants precisely so that adults could ignore them, to his encouragement of home education and the employment of fathers as tutors, demands that parents attend more closely to their children than was then expected, or desired.

Some scholars have argued that Lockean education simply recapitulates the fashions and customs of society at large, but the sheer amount of time that parents will have to spend with their children to the *exclusion* of other company ensures that the family will form its own opinions and judgments *against* those of the society at large.[13] Such resistance is buttressed by the ongoing experience of many years of each other's company. If they were vulgar and beholden to fashion before their children arrived, Lockean parenthood on a rural country estate will tend to sever parents' ties to high society, replacing it with the society of their household and village, and by putting them in the constant presence of their children, urge them to rethink and moderate the unbecoming qualities that may have been prized by their adult companions. Children imitate those they admire, and this very tendency is a check on parents: "You must do nothing before him, which you would not have him imitate" (*STCE* 71). All this in turn fosters a distinct family culture that diverges from the main currents of fashion and public opinion.

Moreover, children themselves will be partial authors of this family culture both because of the insular conditions in which they are brought up, and because they are to engage in frequent conversation with their parents conducted as if between equals, with a father "advis[ing] only as a friend of more experience," particularly about matters directly concerning the family, like the management

---

[13] Ruth Grant points out that the experience of raising children according to Locke's pedagogy helps adults "develop the ability to resist, when necessary, this need for social approval which provides the foundational support for the dominion of custom or 'fashion.' Bravery is required to challenge prevailing views." Grant, "Custom's Power and Reason's Authority," *Review of Politics* 74 (2012): 614.

of the estate (*STCE* 96–97). The obedience imposed in early child-hood becomes the "reasoning with children" of middle childhood (*STCE* 81). This is when negotiation and compromise become pos-sible, and the child's judgments may begin to be incorporated into the family's determinations. Even where children's judgments fall short of prudence, Locke advises parents that, "You must not expect his inclinations should be just as yours...youth must have some lib-erty, some outleaps" (*STCE* 97). Discussing family questions with an older child "will not at all lessen your authority, but increase his love and esteem of you" (*STCE* 97).

Parents can become authoritative sources of esteem and dis-grace for their children only by being admirable to them, so estab-lishing authority requires parents to develop self-mastery as much as their children. Parenting thus turns out to be one of the best ways for "grown men" to "enlarge their understandings," which is other-wise "seldom done" (*CU* 6).[14] By manipulating parents as well as their children, Locke aims not only to form children well but also to improve badly-formed adults, who must be taught how to exercise their authority correctly at least as much as children must be made to submit to it. The home and family are the only plausible setting for such an education, since schools undermine nearly every condi-tion Locke requires: consistent adult authorities who are numerically superior to children, deeply personally invested in the moral and philosophical outcome of their education, and relatively isolated from diversions and competing social influences—that is, protected from the influence of fashion and opinion.

Nonetheless, the *Education* does not aim at a society of perma-nently isolated families living in eccentric worlds of their own, dis-connected from the broader civil society. Locke understands that even "the milder sort of government" which he enjoins on older children is likely to become ineffectual in adolescence, "that boiling

---

[14] Citations to *CU* are to section number in the second work of the following edition: John Locke, *Some Thoughts Concerning Education* and *On the Conduct of the Understanding*, eds. Nathan Tarcov and Ruth Grant (In-dianapolis: Hackett, 1996).

boisterous part of life" when boys chafe under even the most lovable parents' rule, and when they "think themselves too much men to be governed by others, and yet have not prudence and experience enough to govern themselves" (*STCE* 43, 212). It is at this point that children become most susceptible to fashion because they grow skeptical of the familial judgments that had up to then shielded them.

> What can be hoped from even the most careful and discreet governor, when neither he has power to compel, nor his pupil a disposition to be persuaded; but, on the contrary, has the advice of warm blood, and prevailing fashion, to hearken to the temptations of his companions, just as wise as himself, rather than to the persuasions of his tutor, who is now looked on as the enemy to his freedom? (*STCE* 212).

To temper the dangers of this stage, Locke advises delaying the customary period of travel—at the time usually undertaken in early adolescence—until a later age, when "reason and foresight begin a little to take place" so that children are not exposed to "the greatest dangers of their whole life" abroad among strangers. Even at home though, adolescents are inclined to follow the "the temptations of [their] companions" over the judgments of their parents (*STCE* 212). Nonetheless, such conflicts between family and fashion require the child to choose, and thus to deliberate based on his previous positive experience of his family's judgments, forming an important barrier against unthinking acceptance of "prevailing fashion."

It may seem strange that for all his emphasis on home and family education, Locke would concede its eventual insufficiency. But this is because, despite his deference to parental authority, Locke never conceives it to be total or even very effective. Rather, he permits such extensive authority *because* he understands it to be so weak relative to the competing forces in a liberal society—the rebelliousness of children, and the power of fashion and opinion. Even the most authoritative and insular family, provided it retains basic contact with the broader society, is a weak fence against the overwhelming influence of that society's fashions and opinions. By keeping children out of school and away from the influence of servants and other adults, however, Locke merely delays their exposure to fashion and custom, providing them with a family education that will be a counterweight and source of dissonance when they do finally enter the broader society.

Locke's Influence

Locke was perhaps the first widely-read modern political philosopher to call into question the value of schooling for the sake of liberty, but others soon followed his lead. Jean-Jacques Rousseau, in his 1762 treatise on education, *Emile*, took the same position, and for parallel reasons. Like Locke, Rousseau feared the pernicious moral and intellectual influence of modern society, especially on its younger members. Going further even than Locke, Rousseau refused to see the choice between schooling and "domestic education" as a trade-off. Of "boys raised in colleges and girls raised in convents" he says, "the first lessons that both get...are those of vice; and it is not nature that corrupts them, it is example."[15] While Locke admitted some benefits from sending children away to school, Rousseau saw only moral danger.

Emile's early education is undertaken in almost complete isolation, and Sophie—the more practicable model in the book—remains at home until adulthood. But Rousseau considers the potential consequences of exposure to fashion and opinion: "Take a young man soberly raised in his father's home in the country, and examine him at the moment he arrives in Paris and enters society. You will find that he is right-thinking about decent things and even that his will is as healthy as his reason." But an extended stay there will prove fatal to this health: "Consider the same young man six months later. You will no longer

---

[15] Jean-Jacques Rousseau, *Emile*, trans. Allan Bloom (New York: Basic Books, 1979), 330.

recognize him. The easy talk, the fashionable maxims, the jaunty bearing would cause him to be taken for a different man."[16] Rousseau blames the change on conventionally-educated Parisian boys, who, having themselves already been degraded by their pursuit of each other's esteem, will silently recognize Emile's virtue and resent it. "They want to bring you down to their low level, and they reproach you for letting yourself be governed [by your tutor] only in order to govern you themselves. To set themselves above the alleged prejudices of their fathers, they enslave themselves to those of their comrades," Emile's tutor warns him of his peers.[17] This effect is only more concentrated in the social environment of the school, which as Locke pointed out, subjects children to each other's power, instilling habits of submission to prevailing opinion and offering little to counterbalance that opinion's power.

Since nothing good can come of schooling, education must take place at home, ideally with parents as their children's teachers. Rousseau concedes that parents may seem less attractive for the position than professional pedagogues, but insists that their education is still to be preferred, for its moral if not academic result: "As the true nurse is the mother, the true preceptor is the father…He will be better raised by a judicious and limited father than the cleverest master in the world, for zeal will make up for talent better than talent for zeal."[18] Domestic education is good not only for its pupils, who are shielded from the depredations of society by it, but also for parents, who are brought into closer and more affectionate relations with each other through it:

---

[16] Ibid.

[17] Ibid.

[18] *Emile*, 48. This concession will sound strange to those who recall *Emile* as a story of education by an almost omnicompetent tutor, but Rousseau says in Book I that a tutor is actually a second-best alternative, to be engaged only when mothers and fathers refuse their roles in raising their own children. For a more detailed discussion of Rousseau's intention in Book I, see *Liberal States, Authoritarian Families*, ch. 6.

It makes the father and mother more necessary, dearer to one another; it tightens the conjugal bond between them. When the family is lively and animated, the domestic cares constitute the dearest occupation of the wife and the sweetest enjoyment of the husband.[19]

Like Locke, Rousseau argued for home education as a means of constituting the family and insulating it from the influences of a corrupt regime. In other writings, like the *Social Contract, Discourse on Political Economy*, and *Considerations on the Government of Poland*, he praised public education and severely contracted the role of the family, but those writings depict healthy republics where public opinion both reflects and inculcates civic virtue. In modern commercial states, however, public opinion reflects the debauchery of high society, and so the family and private home education must stand as the last fence against individual corruption.

Adam Smith, influenced by both Locke and Rousseau, offered a more attenuated criticism of schools. His concern was less with the deformation of character from being ruled by other children, than with the dangers—both moral and practical—of taking education too much out of the control of the family. In the *Theory of Moral Sentiments*, he warned against boarding schools because they diminished familial affection and the mutual improvement that such affection encourages: "Respect for you must always impose a very useful restraint upon [your children's] conduct; and respect for them may frequently impose no useless restraint upon your own." Smith allowed that, "From their parent's house they may, with propriety and advantage, go out every day to attend public schools," but insisted that, "their dwelling be always at home...Domestic education is the institution of nature; public education, the contrivance of man. It is surely unnecessary to say, which is likely to be the wisest."[20] Smith leaned on the power of public opinion for the support of his impartial spectator, whose judgments are shaped by prevailing mo-

---

[19] *Emile*, 46.

[20] Adam Smith, *The Theory of Moral Sentiments*, eds. D. D. Raphael and A. L. Macfie (Indianapolis: Liberty Fund, 1982) VI.ii.1.

res, so he had no objection to education that exposed children to these mores. Nonetheless, like Locke, he sought to fortify the affection-based nuclear family as a source of moral education and fulfillment—of that "cordial satisfaction, that delicious sympathy, that confidential openness and ease, which naturally take place in the conversation of those who have lived long and familiarly with one another" in "commercial countries."[21]

The *Wealth of Nations* also cast doubt on public education, but for more practical reasons. When teachers are paid a state salary, they do their jobs poorly, since their pay no longer depends on their performance.

> Those parts of education, it is to be observed, for the teaching of which there are no public institutions, are generally the best taught…The three most essential parts of literary education, to read, write, and account, it still continues to be more common to acquire in private than in public schools.[22]

Smith, following Locke, did argue for a system of tax-funded charity schools providing basic education for the poor, but these were a last resort, not a first choice. Education for everyone else should be left to the discretion of parents.

By the nineteenth century, most liberals accepted the necessity of schools for increasingly democratic societies. Lockean homeschooling was for the landed gentry—families who were not engaged in day-to-day moneymaking and had the leisure to teach their children, or the means to hire someone else to do so. But this class was rapidly shrinking, while the class of those who worked for their livings was rapidly expanding. Universal basic education came be to seen as a precondition for the stability of liberal regimes, as Smith had already seen, and a system of public schooling was the most efficient way to deliver it. But even so, liberal skeptics of the tyranni-

---

[21] Ibid.

[22] Adam Smith, *An Inquiry into the Nature and Causes of the Wealth of Nations*, eds. R. H. Campbell and A. S. Skinner (Indianapolis: Liberty Fund, 1982) V.i.2.

cal potential of schooling remained on both sides of the Atlantic.

Even where there is no political tyrant attempting to control what citizens think and say, all states subsist on prevailing dogmas, the seductive but questionable orthodoxies that Locke called fashion and opinion, and the insertion of these dogmas into a uniform national curriculum would have a similar indoctrinating effect. Thus, in England, where the exceptionally slow creation of a public school system did little to dampen the desire for one, J. S. Mill supported state-funded schooling but objected to the idea that the state should have any say in the curriculum. Mill, himself the recipient of a simultaneously impressive and terrifying home education from his father, worried that,

> A general State education is a mere contrivance for molding people to be exactly like one another: and as the mold in which it casts them is that which pleases the predominant power in the government, whether this be a monarch, a priesthood, an aristocracy, or the majority of the existing generation, in proportion as it is efficient and successful, it establishes a despotism over the mind, leading by natural tendency to one over the body.[23]

Mill's fear was of Tocqueville's "tyranny of the majority," a danger exacerbated by public schools, which, by simply reflecting prevailing opinions, imposed them on the susceptible minds of the young.

The early American republic, however, carried forward Locke's pedagogical ideas in a roundabout way. There, as we have seen, schooling was embraced in both theory and practice, seemingly with no thought to Lockean objections. And yet, on closer examination, we find that a good deal of thought *was* given to them. Even the defenders of schools sometimes found themselves answering Lockean objections. One approach was that of Samuel Knox, the co-winner of the 1795 American Philosophical Society essay contest, who directly answered fears that schools would surround chil-

---

[23] John Stuart Mill, *On Liberty*, ed. Alan Ryan (New York: Penguin, 2007), 119.

dren with unregulated and immoral influences. He insisted that no domestic education was private enough to keep out all temptations, and that bad influences were more likely to fester in the seclusion of private families than amid the variety of a school.[24] Noah Webster compromised with Locke as well, designing schools to approximate as much as possible the environment of the home, locating them in rural villages rather than cities and proposing to board students with "decent families, to be subject, in some measure, to their discipline, and ever under the control of those whom they respect" instead of in dormitories.[25] He defended the "absolute authority" of parents, as Locke did, and extended this authority to schoolteachers as well, whose conduct was to be modeled on benevolent and respectable parents, and whose characters and qualifications must be substantially elevated to meet this standard.[26] Besides, Knox pointed out, even "the celebrated Locke" himself was a beneficiary of institutional schooling, so who was he to complain about it?[27]

Another, ultimately more influential American approach to Locke's criticism of schooling was taken by Benjamin Franklin in his *Autobiography*. Franklin, the youngest son of the seventeen children of a Boston candle maker, understood that Locke's tutorial home education was wholly unsuited to "the manners and situation of [the] rising people" of the nascent United States.[28] But he was also critical of institutional schooling, and proposed instead (or in addition to it) a model of self-education that adapted Locke's liberal insights for democratic exigencies. To signal his own purposes in the book, Franklin inserted into his *Autobiography* a fawning letter from his friend Benjamin Vaughn, praising his writings for,

---

[24] Samuel Knox, *An Essay on the Best System of Liberal Education* (Baltimore: 1799), 64.

[25] Noah Webster, *On the Education of Youth in America* (New York: 1788), 11–12.

[26] Webster, *Education of Youth*, 15–16.

[27] Knox, *Best System*, 65. Locke was educated at Westminster School.

[28] Benjamin Franklin, *Autobiography*, ed. Daniel Aron (New York: Library of America, 1990), 70.

giv[ing] a noble rule and example of self-education. School and other education constantly proceed upon false principles, and shew a clumsy apparatus pointed at a false mark; but your apparatus is simple, and the mark a true one; and while parents and young persons are left destitute of other just means of estimating and becoming prepared for a reasonable course in life, your discovery that the thing is in many a man's private power, will be invalua-ble![29]

These democratic exigencies—the lack of a leisured gentry and the constant occupation of most American parents with making a living and maintaining a household—meant that the home could not be the insular retreat from public opinion that it was for Locke, nor could parents be the sole pedagogical authorities he proposed. Children left unsupervised to raise themselves had great intellectual independence, but also, lacking the discipline that Locke's education would have imposed, faced greater danger from the base temptations of the adult world to which they were constantly exposed. The *Autobiography* offers, in addition to the success story of Franklin's life, cautionary tales of boys like his friend John Collins, who despite their youthful promise, succumbed to drinking and gambling before they could develop their talents.

Franklin's solution was to impose Lockean discipline on himself, and to develop his experience into a system of self-discipline—an "Art of Virtue," as he called it—for others to follow, complete with rules, check-lists, daily schedules. Franklin's self-discipline, like Locke's, subjected him to discomfort and privation to develop self-control, motivated abstract study by its practical benefits, and rejected secondhand beliefs in favor of independent reasoning—so independent that he acquired a reputation as a heretic and had to leave Puritan Boston. The result was a Lockean education without tutors, parents, or much adult authority at all; this was Locke adapted for the American situation.

---

[29] Franklin, *Autobiography*, 71.

Instead of adult authority, Franklin relied on friendships with similarly-situated young men to overcome the constraints of his poverty. Combining with them for mutual improvement in both formal and informal ways, he increased his access to books, found listeners and disputants to vet his philosophical and civic ideas, and created what we would today describe as a professional network whose members helped each other to advance in their careers as they grew more established themselves. Self-education through voluntary association—clubs, fraternal organizations, and civic undertakings—was Franklin's central workaround for an essentially democratic society of families too poor and busy for Locke's home education.[30] Children's intellectual independence could be preserved not by sheltering them from outside influences, but by making them individually the authors of their own educations, including a component that required them to sift through other children for like-minded compatriots and to learn to cooperate with them for mutual advancement. Self-education and association were mutually-reinforcing: he called the Junto, an informal debating society made up of small tradesmen interested in philosophy and civic improvement, "the best School of Philosophy, Morals & Politics that then existed in the Province."[31] Better, that is, than any institutional school.

Franklin's modification of Locke's pedagogy had a lasting impact on American educational philosophy, which to this day retains a suspicion of schooling unusual among developed nations, even as institutional schooling has become nearly-universal practice. Franklin's compromise was to accept that the new republic must have schools, but to deny that all or even most of what we understand as *education* would occur in them. He inaugurated a tradition of Amer-

---

[30] The almost comical rule-boundedness of Franklin's associations—each one has what amounts to its own constitution, and he devotes a good deal of attention to their provisions—distinguish them from the more tyrannical and anti-Lockean ways that groups of unsupervised children tend to associate, which are exemplified by the informal street gang, a fixture of American urban life since the eighteenth century, but certainly not Franklin's aim.

[31] Franklin, *Autobiography*, 58.

ican thinking about education that accepted the democratic necessity of public schooling, but retained the Lockean suspicion of its stifling moral and intellectual effects. And so it did for many years. Even for the growing number of children attending school as the common school movement gained traction, the world outside of it—of unschooled summers (and, for many years and many children, also autumns and springs), unsupervised adventures with friends, and livelihoods not dependent on institutional imprimatur—limited the moral and intellectual influence of the school. The result was not Locke's home education, but the important American move was to *substitute* self-education for home education, in an effort to preserve the same goal—intellectual liberty—by different means.

Conclusion: Maybe Homeschooling

Taken together, the logic of Locke's anti-institutional argument is clear: send your child to school and he will be governed there not by exemplary pedagogical authorities, but by other children, who are as ignorant as yours but, in large numbers, much more vicious. The moral authority of the peer group over the individual child is nearly omnipotent, but it is wielded tyrannically. As Hannah Arendt described the problem centuries later,

> The authority of a group, even a child group, is always considerably stronger and more tyrannical than the severest authority of an individual person can be...By being emancipated from the authority of adults the child has not been freed but has been subjected to a much more terrifying and truly tyrannical authority, the tyranny of the majority.[32]

Children are tyrants to one another, demanding extravagant conformity, no matter how arbitrary or vicious the object. Keeping children away from the child group and under the benevolent authority of parents or other adults hand-selected by parents at home

---

[32] Hannah Arendt, "The Crisis in Education," in *Between Past and Future* (New York: Penguin, 1968), 181.

permits them to develop their characters away from such corrosive temptations, but reinforces the virtue of parents as well as children, as both strive to be held in high regard by the other.

According to Locke and those influenced by him, the structure of the school—with its too-numerous pupils and the questionable influence of its teachers—threatens the eventual intellectual liberty of the child by exposing him too intensively and continuously to the authority of fashion and opinion. Contrary to the common view of Americans today, it is schooling, not homeschooling, that results in social maladjustment, at least if we take intellectual independence to be the standard of social adjustment. But pathology is much harder to see or acknowledge when it is the predominant way of being. For many years, following the tradition inaugurated by Franklin, Americans tried to strike a balance, to benefit from the goods of schooling—a cheap and reliable source of literacy and basic moral instruction—while minimizing its overall influence on the experience of childhood. But its influence grew, and at the same time as direct community control of its operations diminished. When the modern homeschooling movement arose in the 1960s, one conviction that united its quite disparate members was precisely that contemporary mass schooling had become too omnipotent in children's lives and had turned into exactly what Mill feared—a source of indoctrination.[33]

Today, we tend to assume the opposite, that indoctrination is much more likely to come from the home, where the parochial worldview of a few adults prevails, rather than a school, which contains a multiplicity of viewpoints. Indeed, we often see it as the job of the school to compensate for the narrowness of parental upbringing or even undo its damage in order to ensure the production of good liberal citizens.[34] But perhaps we have the situation backwards.

---

[33] Milton Gaither, *Homeschool: An American History* (New York: Palgrave, 2016), ch. 4.

[34] This is the argument of many contemporary liberal and democratic theorists of education, including Amy Gutmann, Meira Levinson, Stephen Macedo, and others. For a fuller overview of this argument, see Rita

In the history of Western political thought, after all, it is over-whelmingly liberals rather than conservatives who have been skeptical of schooling.

Locke hardly feared the distorting or too-parochial influence of the family on the child because, just beyond it, he saw the much more encompassing and compelling influence of public opinion, especially consolidated under a strong central government. Without any counterweights, that influence would soon insinuate itself of its own accord via children's natural moral weakness and desperate desire for other people's approval. Even the isolated, rural families Locke imagined were part of a larger society whose influence would penetrate into the home—through parents' youthful experiences, books and visitors, and especially through the eventuality of the children's growing up and leaving. Against the enormous influence that social pressures and our own raw and untrained desires exert against free thought, Locke saw the irrational eccentricities of particular families as a minor inconvenience rather than a threat to liberal citizenship.

As Locke himself understood, there are good democratic reasons that his home education cannot be universal in an "all middle class" country.[35] But as his followers also understood, even as they accepted the necessity of schooling, the philosophical danger that he saw in it is not answered by its economic or social necessity. But Locke's original anti-schooling arguments have largely been forgotten as universal public schooling took root in the US and Europe. In recovering them, we might want to reconsider our popular and academic prejudices against homeschooling. Rather than accepting institutional education as the universal norm, and home education as a bizarre deviation, Locke illuminates ways in which it is schooling that distorts children's characters and intellects. Now, for the first time in well over a century, the majority of American families will

Koganzon, "Educating for Liberty? Teachers and Civic Education," in *The Professions and Civic Life*, ed. Gary Schmitt (Lexington Books, 2016).

[35] His proposal for workhouse schools for the poor in his "Essay on the Poor Law" (1697) makes this clear.

have personally experienced some version of home education, however attenuated by the distressing circumstances of the pandemic.

It is too early to say with any certainty how many of them will continue homeschooling after districts re-open. Early findings indicate that most families who switched over to homeschooling during the pandemic intend to stick with it, which could push the percentage of children being homeschooled in the US up substantially, as high as 10 percent.[36] But perhaps the liberal educational philosophy that grew out of Locke's pedagogy does not require a nation of homeschoolers. What it might require, however, is that we see the close relationship between a certain kind of intensive and highly personal pedagogical authority over children and their eventual freedom, and the degree to which such authority is most easily and perhaps naturally cultivated in the family. While much of the public discussion about our recent unintended experiment in national homeschooling has focused on its challenges, some families have reported that their children seemed remarkably happier out of school, less tired and anxious, and relieved to have escaped the unrelenting social pressures and constant scrutiny by their peers.[37] Per-

---

[36] According to the US Census, 11.1 percent of families reported homeschooling in Fall 2020, and anecdotal evidence alongside continued enrollment declines in public schools as the 2021–22 school year begins suggest that a substantial proportion of those families may stick with it. Casey Eggleston and Jason Fields, "Census Bureau's Household Pulse Survey Shows Significant Increase in Homeschooling Rates in Fall 2020" US Census Bureau Household Pulse Survey, 22 March 2021. https://www.census.gov/library/stories/2021/03/homeschooling-on-the-rise-during-covid-19-pandemic.html; Belsha, LeMee, Fenn, and Ma, "After enrollment dips, America's schools hope for fall rebound" Chalkbeat, 26 June 2021. https://www.chalkbeat.org/2021/6/16/22529686/schools-student-enrollment-decline-white-hispanic-fall-2021.

[37] Since we do not yet have the benefit of more systematic hindsight, we must rely for the time being on anecdotal accounts, e.g.: Joanna Schroeder, "What if Some Kids Are Better Off at Home?" *New York Times*, 10 August 2020; Melody Warnick, "Not Everyone Hates School at Home," *New York Times*, 16 July 2020; Meghan Leahy, "My kids seem happier since the pandemic slowed life down. Should I be worried?" *Wash-*

haps it will not be such a bad thing in the long run to experience Locke's argument so viscerally.

ington Post, 5 August 2020; Emma Green, "The Pandemic Has Parents Fleeing From Schools—Maybe Forever," *The Atlantic*, 13 September 2020; Natasha Singer, "Online Schools are Here to Stay, Even After the Pandemic," The New York Times, 11 April 2021.

6

IS LOCKE A CONTRACTUAL THINKER ON MARRIAGE?

Scott Yenor

Let me cut to the chase. Locke *is* a contractual thinker when it comes to marriage. The larger question however is whether he is a contractual thinker as we today understand a contractual thinker. Locke's understanding of what the marital contract entails may indeed be superior to our understanding of what the marital contract entails. There is even a Lockean critique of our understanding of the marital contract. I plan on first laying out the elements of the marriage contract in the terms of contemporary liberalism, then to contrast our understanding of the marriage contract with Locke's, and lastly to show how Locke would criticize the contemporary liberal understanding.

This may seem like a semantic debate. But I fancy that it is a semantic debate with real implications for our understanding of a liberal polity—and the place of the family and marriage within it. There is a common critique of modern, Lockean liberalism and of the American Founders that includes the following line of argument.[1] The United States is ill founded because it is grounded in individual rights. Initially, at least, the mostly Christian environment encouraged the public-spirited, responsible exercise of individual rights; its Lockean principles were thus contained in what Peter Lawler called "the Locke box."[2] As the Christian heritage fad-

---

[1] Patrick Deneen, *Why Liberalism Failed* (New Haven: Yale University Press, 2018) is the most famous recent iteration of this argument.

[2] Lawler refers the Locke box in numerous publications. See "Dogmatic Straussians," *First Things* (January 27, 2013), retrieved June 18, 2021

ed or was consumed by the principles of modern individualism, the principles of individual autonomy came to remake familial and marital institutions. The only legitimate principle for establishing marital life, for example, became consent. If today's idea of marriage is the inescapable and logical working out of Locke's ideas, then his more moderate contractarian approach presages an inevitable corruption and his reservations about today's ideas are bound to yield to the more radical approach. All contracts, the argument goes, must eventually be based on the private contract, especially when private contracts in the market place are so common. By private contract, I mean an agreement between two or more people without anyone or anything shaping the consent of either party; only the private individuals are party to the contract. So, at stake here is "what do we mean by contract?" and "how do we determine what is and what is not a better understanding of a contract?"

Let me propose two or three words of caution about the school of thought that sees an inevitability in the move from John Locke and George Washington to same-sex marriage and beyond. There is a logic to the argument to be sure (namely, that the emphasis on individual rights eventually wears away restraints on them), but the development of human society is not simply a matter of logic. First, every trend in American family life is present in Europe and in Asia too—declining marriage rates, more cohabitation, low birth rates, more divorce, later marriage, and so on. Nearly all these countries have total fertility rates below replacement level.[3] The fact that this

---

at   https://www.firstthings.com/blogs/firstthoughts/2013/01/dogmatic-straussians.

[3] Consider especially the issue of falling birth rates, related to other forms of family decline and marital collapse. See Philip Longman, *The Empty Cradle: How Falling Birthrates Threaten World Prosperity (and What to Do About It)* (Cambridge, MA: Perseus Group, 2004); Nicholas Eberstadt, "The Demographic Future: What Population Growth—and Decline—Mean for The Global Economy," *Foreign Affairs* 89 (2010): 54–64; David P. Goldman, *How Civilizations Die (And Why Islam Is Dying Too),* (Washington D.C.: Regnery, 2011) esp. 1–26; Jonathan Last, *What to Expect When No One's Expecting: America's Coming Demographic Disaster* (New

is a global phenomenon means that the overall trajectory is not traceable to a country's particular situation or any country's peculiar ideology or complex of laws. The nearly universal nature of this decline provides food for reflection about the nature of human being itself.[4] If the same trends are happening in more communitarian countries as well as "individualistic" countries, then the presence or absence of a tradition of Lockean individual rights may not be implicated in family decline and marriage decline.

Second, the particular timing of the American transformation would need to be explained. It is strange to blame a man whose writings appeared in the late 1600s for *today's* problems or to hold the inventor of the modern family—one of the most enduring family forms in history—for its demise. Why did it take roughly eight generations from the establishment of the liberal American polity until the victory of deracinated individualism? Further, it is reasonable to ask what political system, and what family system, holds up in the very long run. The seeds for the destruction of all or most human arrangements are often sown in their founding principles. No

---

York: Encounter Books, 2013); and more academic treatments such as Ann Buchanan and Anna Rotkirtch eds., *Fertility Rates and Population Decline: No Time for Children?* (New York: Palgrave MacMillan, 2013) and Noriyuki Takayama and Martin Werding eds., *Fertility and Public Policy: How to Reverse the Trend of Declining Birthrates* (Cambridge, MA: MIT Press, 2011).

[4] Consider the following from Immanuel Kant's "Idea for a Universal History with a Cosmopolitan Intent," *Perpetual Peace and Other Essays*, translated by Ted Humphrey (Indianapolis, IN: Hackett, 1983), 29: "Since the free wills of men seem to have so great an influence on marriage, the births consequent to it, and death, it appears that they are not subject to any rule by which one can in advance determine their number; and yet the annual charts that large countries make of them show that they occur in conformity with natural laws as invariable as those governing the unpredictable weather, whose particular changes we cannot determine in advance, but which in the large do not fail to support a uniform and uninterrupted pattern in the growth of plants, in the flow of rivers, and in other natural events."

family form is permanently stable.⁵ When Locke wrote, he faced some of the problems associated with today's family decline (poor marriage formation, incompetent parenting, divorce⁶) and may have anticipated others (associated with feminism). Those praising Locke are impressed with his declaration that marriage accomplishes important natural and seemingly unchangeable ends, namely the procreation and education of children, and that some family forms accomplish these ends better than others.

So how direct is the line from Locke to contemporary liberalism on the family? Can Locke be blamed for putting modern civilization on the trajectory that led to family decline?

Section 1: Contemporary Liberalism— Marital Contract without Public Involvement

Let us start with contemporary liberalism. The watchwords for contemporary liberalism on marriage are consent and state neutrality. Marriages must be founded on consent and can end through consent. Neutrality demands that the state must not favor any kind of marital arrangement over others. Ultimately, these concepts point to the state retreating from the realm of marriage and thinking of marriage as a contract just like any other, where the parties themselves are the only ones who "negotiate" its terms. This amounts to privatizing marriage—and privatizing marriage has two principal attributes.

First, the most radical iteration of privatizing marriage is that, absent a contract, the state takes no cognizance of adult relationships. Adult marriage-like relationships are not part of the social

---

⁵ See Carle C. Zimmerman, *Family and Civilization*, edited by James Kurth (Wilmington, DE: ISI Press, 2008).

⁶ See Peter Laslett, *Family-Life and Illicit Love in Earlier Generations* (Cambridge: Cambridge University Press, 1977), 102–159; Gordon Schochet, *The Authoritarian Family and Political Attitudes in 17ᵗʰ Century England* (New York: Transaction, 1987), 54–84; and Lawrence Stone, *The Family, Sex and Marriage in England, 1500–1800* (New York: Harper & Row, 1977), 628–636, 645–648.

contract. They remain outside the notice of civil government, akin to friendships. They are open as to number in the marriage, sexuality, duration, depth, practice of fidelity, purpose, and extent of sharing. Whether they are a couple, a "throuple," or something else; whether they are gay or straight; whether members are faithful or not; whether they be monogamous parents of six children, swingers, traditional polygamists, or other forms of "complex marriage"—the state recognizes only individuals and cannot even recognize marital contracts as distinguished from other contracts.[7]

Second, privatizing marriage requires government to refrain from promoting and supporting marriage and parenthood. While it is difficult to describe all that this involves, any law that has as its chief justification the maintenance of mores that support marriage would immediately be suspect among those seeking to privatize marriage. Laws prohibiting prostitution, pornography, and public nudity, for instance, might lose their *raison d'etre* under these circumstances, for such laws exist mostly to guide people's actions and ideas concerning proper sexual relations and point people to devoted monogamous relations. Any law attempting to support more directly a monogamous, faithful vision of marriage—either promoting it through public education or incentivizing it with public benefits—runs afoul of the demand to privatize marriage.

Generally, those who would privatize marriage *as far as possible* do so in the name of fundamental aspirations such as equality, indi-

---

[7] See especially the following libertarian writings on the family and marriage: David Boaz, "Privatize Marriage," Cato.org (April 1997). Accessed November 4, 2019, https://www.cato.org/publications/commentary/privatize-marriage; Wendy McElroy, "The Grayness of Children's Rights," *Daily Anarchist* (September 14, 2012) accessed June 19, 2021, http://dailyanarchist.com/2012/09/11/the-grayness-of-childrens-rights; and Murray Rothbard, *The Ethics of Liberty* (New York: New York University Press, 1998), 100–102. For a treatment of the contemporary liberal approach to marriage, see Scott Yenor, *The Recovery of Family Life: Exposing the Limits of Modern Ideologies* (Waco: Baylor University Press, 2020), 43–57.

vidual independence, and autonomy.[8] According to contemporary liberals, public law about marriage cannot support any controversial ideas about marital form, matter, or character. Should marriage be enduring, permanent, or at will? The law cannot say. Should marriage be for the purposes of procreation and education of children or adult-fulfillment? The law cannot say. Should marriage be essentially heterosexual? The law cannot say. Should people living together be married or is living together without the piece of paper sufficient for public recognition? The law cannot say. Ultimately, the question becomes "should there be marriage?" The law, under contemporary liberalism, cannot even say "yes."

This explains the tendency manifest in contemporary liberal iterations of family teachings either to minimize marriage[9] or abolish marriage as a legal category.[10] With apologies to Alexander Pope: whether minimizing marriage amounts to its abolition let fools contest; all arguments in support of marriage on contemporary liberal grounds fail the test. No one pays attention to this as the ultimate goal of contemporary liberalism, but this goal is present and it is the implicit teaching of all contemporary liberal efforts to re-make the

---

[8] See Linda McClain, *The Place of Families* (Cambridge: Harvard University Press, 2006), 217, who would maintain marriage, among other similar reasons, for the "expressive benefit of public recognition of—and validation of—their commitment"; and Elizabeth Brake, *Minimizing Marriage* (New York: Oxford University Press, 2012) 174ff. Brake emphasizes the social support for caring relationships that extend marriage well beyond the heterosexual dyad to both homosexuals and to groups; and Ronald C. Den Otter, *In Defense of Plural Marriage* (New York: Cambridge University Press, 2015), 80–89 and 103–107.

[9] See, for example, Brake, *Minimizing Marriage*.

[10] Examples of those who would abolish marriage as a legal category include Sophie Lewis, *Full Surrogacy Now: Feminism Against the Family* (London: Verso, 2019); Tamara Metz, *Untying the Knot: Marriage, the State, and the Case for their Divorce* (Princeton University Press, 2010), 115; Martha Fineman, *The Autonomy Myth: A Theory of Dependency* (London: New Press, 2005), 123; and Steve Vanderheiden, "Why the State Should Stay out of the Wedding Chapel," *Public Affairs Quarterly* 13, no. 2 (1999): 175–199.

family. If this is what Locke has in mind, then his liberalism is bound to lead to the abolition of the family.

Section 2: Locke's Contractual Marriage

But the abolition of the family is not necessarily what Locke has in mind, and the fact that Locke's own teaching on this lasted for three hundred years, more or less, suggests that Locke's teaching on family appeals to several relatively stable challenges of nature, and there are only a certain number of ways to meet those challenges. The most crucial difference between Locke's idea of contract and today's concerns the status of the public. It is our job to figure out the reason for this different status of the public. While today's liberals seek a state neutrality on the nature of marriage, Locke explicitly imagines civil government shaping and enforcing the purpose of the marriage contract and hence also the terms of it. The public gets involved because marriage deals with inescapable natural challenges—the long minority of children and the differences between men and women.

Locke is a well-known critic of patriarchal rule, but he first sees patriarchy as an accomplishment and then as a problem. Let us trace his thinking here as a way of understanding his insistence that the public play a role in designing marriage.

Families are rooted in natural, biological facts, and marriage deals with those facts. As with many animals, man and woman come together for "Procreation" and the "continuation of the Species" (2T 79).[11] Unlike many other newborn animals, children are

---

[11] I refer to Locke's works by the following abbreviations and editions: *First Treatise of Government=1T* (followed by section number); *Second Treatise= 2T* (followed by section); *Essay Concerning Human Understanding=ECHU* (followed by book, chapter, and section); and *Some Thoughts Concerning Education=STCE* (followed by section). The editions used are these: *Two Treatises of Government*, Edited by Peter Laslett (Cambridge University Press, 1960); *Essay Concerning Human Understanding*, 2 Volumes (Dover, 1959); and *Some Thoughts Concerning Education*, Edited by Ruth Grant (Hackett, 1996).

dependent on parents for continued care, which explains why men and women need to be "tied to a longer conjunction than other creatures" (*2T* 80). Marriages and families are therefore artificial and political institutions designed to answer the natural needs of children.

In addition to the problem of children there is the problem of males. Mothers, it seems, as Locke treats the matter, feel attached to children, inducing them to provide affectionate care for their off-spring, yet men do not by nature seem interested in being husbands or fathers or in having other long-term commitments. "What Father of a Thousand," Locke asks, "when he begets a Child, thinks farther than satisfying his present Appetite?" So little are men interested in family life that God found it necessary to place "strong desires of Copulation" in men to confound them into perpetuating the race. Sexual desire leads men to beget children "without the intention, and often against the Consent and the Will of the Begetter" (*1T* 54). As men pursue fleeting desires, "the Husband and Wife part"—that is, the husband *de*parts—and the "Children are left to the Mother, follow her, and are whole under her Care and Provision." Easy and "frequent Solutions of Conjugal society. . .mightily disturb" the provision of children, as does an "uncertain mixture" leading to conception (*2T* 65 and 80), and such events are common in primitive America and other locales. Far from beginning his analysis by identifying the problem of patriarchy and partisanship, Locke begins with the primitive problem of "Fatherless America" or "Life Without Father."[12] Nor is it necessarily best if primitive men stick around. Locke catalogues the "sports of men"—including incidents of cannibalism, child sacrifice, exposure, feeding children to wild beasts, and burying children alive—when they are freed from

---

[12] David Blankenhorn, *Fatherless America* (New York: HarperCollins, 1996); and David Popenoe, *Life Without Father* (New York: The Free Press, 1996). This "male problematic" is a hallmark of the contemporary literature on socio-biology. See especially David Buss, *The Evolution of Desire* (New York: Basic Books, 1975) and Scott Yenor, *Family Politics: The Idea of Marriage in Modern Political Thought* (Waco: Baylor University Press, 2011) Chapter 10.

law and censure (*ECHU* 1.3.9).[13] Neither the meandering nor malevolent man constitutes a civilized and civilizing family. Man must first be "tamed" or brought into the great project of civilization before any family life can be experienced.

Patriarchy is therefore an accomplishment of sorts that meets natural needs and that solves the problem of the wandering, uncivilized man—in a manner of speaking. It also creates a new slew of problems in itself. Women seem to consent to patriarchy as a survival strategy, receiving protection, help, and support from men in return for granting men access to sex and control over the family and its property. Political society emerges after stable, mostly patriarchal families form. Patriarchy is an accomplishment, but by creating a new set of problems patriarchy itself needs to be limited. As a matter of fact, paternal power exceeds these limits set by parental rule; paternal rule is taken as proof that God intends fathers to be kings. More significant are the cultural problems of patriarchy. Patriarchy is defined by a complex of opinions, many of which are central to the Christian, ancient, and medieval traditions.[14] The central goal of this tradition is for children to learn obedience to something greater than, and outside, themselves. Fathers are charged with training a child's will, so that the honor children should show to fathers is preparation for the honor all owe to God and all citizens

---

[13] See also *1T* 54–56.

[14] What follows in this paragraph borrows from David Foster, "Taming the Father," *The Review of Politics*, vol. 56, no. 4 (Fall 1994): 664–667. As representatives of the tradition, consider John Calvin, *Institutes of the Christian Religion*, 2 Volumes, translated by Henry Beveridge (Grand Rapids, MI.: Eerdmans, 1957), II.viii.35–38; Robert Filmer, *Patriarcha and Other Writings*, edited by Johann Sommerville (Cambridge: Cambridge University Press, 1991), 12; Samuel Pufendorf, *On the Duty of Man and Citizen According to Natural Law*, Edited by James Tully and Translated by Michael Silverthorne (Cambridge: Cambridge University Press, 1991), 126–7; Aristotle, *Nicomachean Ethics*, translated by Robert C. Bartlett and Susan D. Collins (Chicago: University of Chicago Press, 2011), 1163b15–29; and Cicero, *De Officiis*, translated by Walter Miller (Cambridge: Loeb Classical Library, 1913), xvii.

owe to established governments. Just as fearing the Lord is the beginning of wisdom, so also is fearing one's Father and Mother essential to a Christian education.

The fact that patriarchy is sustained by closely supervised opinions about obedience reveals much about human nature. Locke is often associated with the view that human beings are possessive or anti-social because he envisions man alone and hungry in the state of nature. Yet it is best to see Locke's emphasis on the individual as a counterpoise to man's predominantly and anxiously *social* nature— a social nature that makes human beings vulnerable to tribal and familial attachments. One would have to be, Locke writes, "little skilled in nature or history of mankind" to miss the fact that the greatest part of mankind "govern themselves chiefly, if not solely, by this *law of fashion*" (*ECHU* 2.28.12). The desire for esteem being natural to man, it is also "natural for [him], and almost unavoidable, to take up with some borrowed principles. . . from his education and from the fashions of his country" (*ECHU* 1.3.26). Thinking through the way people borrow principles reveals that the family is the agent that gives them to children. Children come into the world anxious, desiring to please others, and ready to be impressed with a character; parents get the first stab at molding character while children are at their most pliable. Children recognize an inequality between themselves and their fathers and this inequality has great political importance—it fosters obedience. It also has great importance for the family. Children are taught to prefer their family to outsiders; they are indoctrinated to the family's religious opinions, which can reinforce opinions about kingship, obedience, and a suspicion about the other. Children lose their independence of judgment before they are allowed to cultivate it, and this "giving up our assent to the common received opinions, either of our friends or party, neighbourhood or country" (*ECHU* 4.20.17) is the chief source of all intellectual errors and also of great injustices.

Locke therefore finds it necessary to create a bit of distance between children and parents. The purpose of this is to limit natural human partisanship. Locke reforms the family by stripping away layers of custom that reinforce patriarchal rule while asking men and women to revisit the survival strategy underlying the patriarchal family. His aim is to keep the stability of the patriarchal family while limiting the patriarchy. Will ending the culture of patriarchy return us to a more natural time of the wandering male and the abandoned woman and child? Not out of an attempt to escape nature, but rather from a hope to better satisfy its demands, Locke seeks to defang patriarchy and re-constitute the family. Can the givens of nature—the facts that children are long dependent on mothers and that mothers have long, somewhat debilitating gestation periods—be satisfied without resorting to patriarchy, its partisanship, and its tendency to political absolutism? Is there any stable middle ground between Robert Filmer and John Rawls, or between the distorting injustice of patriarchal families and tribes and the atomizing families of today?

Locke's answer to these challenges involves establishing public institutions that channel natural desires into publicly useful directions. The desire for self-preservation in men, the "strong desires for Copulation" in men, the caring disposition in women, the weakness and vulnerability in women, and the long nonage of children all call out for an institution to manage the problem. Nature provides the materials and the challenge: Locke's version of the contractual family manages them. Conjugal society "is made by a voluntary compact between Man and Woman" consisting in "such Communion and right in one another's bodies, as is necessary to its chief End, Procreation" (2T 78). These natural "givens" limit human power, creativity, and freedom, insofar as they are "givens."

Let us begin with a strict constructionist view of Locke's understanding of marriage. When Locke defends a form of the family, he puts forward an institution—a complex of rules, expectations, and *mores*—that make a law of fashion to structure how people think and act. In Locke's definition of conjugal society, all the essentials of Locke's marriage institution emerge. First, it begins in "a voluntary compact" or consent. Consent guarantees, insofar as possible, the sentiments necessary for a conjugal society to perform its tasks of procreation and education. Consent to marry is evidence of a willingness to provide "mutual Support, and Assistance" and to signify a "Communion of Interest too, as necessary. . .to unite their Care, and Affection" (*2T* 78). Consensual marriage *recognizes* sentiments and passions as essential, if not *the* essential, traits of married and private life. Second, marriage is lasting, if not permanent. Consistent with his account of marriage's ends, Locke allows that marriages can be terminated once their child-centered goals are accomplished (*2T* 81). Third, and most crucially, marriage is an institution that emphasizes *connections* between form and function. In this particular case, Locke sees connections between sex and procreation, marriage and procreation, marriage and parenthood, and the education of children and parenthood.

The question about institutions with certain characteristics is whether the connections connect what they purport to connect. Locke's argument has two steps: first, conjugal society is necessary, or at least important to and convenient for, the education of children; and second, the family's goal of educating children is necessary for a child's independent entry into adulthood and political society. The necessity for this institution, as Locke understands it, arises from the natural facts that children are born to a prolonged state of dependence, more children often arrive before the first ones fly the coop, and two complementary parents can have children and are better equipped to raise them well. The nuclear family is the human institution that best satisfies natural necessities. Men and women combine resources, unite interests, and "make Provision" to sustain each other and educate their "common Issue" (*2T* 79). Marriage serves the family and must maintain a suitable form to do so.

Locke does not unqualifiedly defend each of these attributes or connections in his teaching. Locke implies that divorce is permissible, for example, when minor children are still at home. The contract could determine if the "Children upon such Separation fall to the Father or Mother's Lot." "Natural Right, or their Contract" determines when such a separation can occur (*2T* 82). The "natural Right" implicated in divorce is likely the preservation of the wife and children, which overrides one's duty to remain in a marriage when threatened by an abusive husband. Though Locke does not expand on this point, he suggests that the civil magistrate can dissolve marriages for non-performance of contract, perhaps if one fails to allow access to "one anothers Bodies," or to provide the "mutual Support, and Assistance whilst they are together," or to guard, nourish, educate, and support one's child. The civil magistrate decides "any Controversie that may arise between Man and Wife" about the terms of their marital contract (*2T* 78, 83, 65). Neither whim nor subjective will apart from evidence of a breach of contract nor one party pure and simple can dissolve a marriage.[15] The fashion Locke cultivates is that marriages should endure, except where they should not (because of a breach or abuse) or need not (for the sake of the children). But marriage can dissolve.

Locke is also not very dogmatic on how business within the family should operate. Locke maintains a softer, privatized patriarchy as he gives headship of families to the "abler and stronger" man (*2T* 82), to the consternation of many.[16] But this soft patriarchy is hemmed in and not essential to marriage and family life; it is not sown into its very nature and definition. It is ultimately an empirical question whether patriarchy is necessary to maintain family life. Consider the following aspects of Locke's teaching. Men rule as abler and stronger persons, not as men. Locke's family is thus open to claims from superior women since he justifies rule on the basis of a kind of merit, not sex. He also writes this:

> Community of goods, and the power over them, mutual assistance and maintenance, and other things belonging to conjugal society, might be varied and regulated by that contract which unites man and wife in that society, as far

---

[15] Peter Myers, *Only Star and Compass* (Lanham, MD: Rowman & Littlefield, 1996), 205–206.

[16] See Melissa Butler, "Early Liberal Roots of Feminism: John Locke's Attack on Patriarchy," in *Feminist Interpretations of John Locke*, edited by Nancy J. Hirschmann and Kristie M. McClure (College Station: Pennsylvania State University Press, 2007), 105; Mary Lyndon Shanley, "Marriage Contract and Social Contract," in *Feminist Interpretations of John Locke*, 90–95; and Carole Pateman, *The Sexual Contract* (Palo Alto: Stanford University Press, 1988), Chapter 4.

as may consist with procreation and the bringing up of children till they could shift for themselves; nothing being necessary to any society, that is not necessary to the ends for which it is made. (*2T* 83)

If and so long as the husband's rule is necessary to procreation and the education of the young, husbandly rule in the family stands. If not, rule in the family may be negotiated between rational, independent, and equal parties entering the contract. If previously it was necessary to give men rule of the family as part of a strategy to keep them around, another strategy could be devised so long as the end is still met. Where parents do not seem to be subject to "Magistrates power," controversies between husbands and wives can be appealed to "the Civil Magistrate" (*1T* 64). This ambiguous entrée of the magistrate in marital controversies qualifies the rule of the husband, as does the fact that Locke allows for divorce after the marriage's terms are fulfilled and, perhaps, when one does not keep up one's end of the bargain. Locke is open to women owning property, bequeathing inheritance, receiving an education similar to a man's, and possessing the rationality necessary for citizenship.[17] The principles Locke plants in the family can reform it again, depending on the circumstances.

Yet the connections at the heart of Locke's marital institution are indeed quite connected. The chain of connections from sex to procreation to marriage to parenthood to education is quite durable. In this, Locke soberly submits to stubborn facts (i.e., the neediness of children and the differences between men and women). The sta-

---

[17] Consider especially his comments on the education of girls: "I will take the Liberty to say, that. . . the nearer they come to the Hardships of their Brothers in their Education, the greater Advantage will they receive from it all the remaining Part of their Lives" (*STCE* 9). That Locke is no simple patriarch or that his teaching in this regard is open to feminist development or even that Locke is not fully candid about the full and liberating implications of conceiving of marriage as a contract between equals is the emphasis of a whole strand of arguments, including Myers, *Only Star and Compass*, 202; and Butler, "Early Liberal Roots of Feminism," 115–118.

bility of Locke's family derives from his ability to identify enduring natural facts and his willingness to grasp their implications. Meanwhile, Locke debunks institutions that were mistakenly thought to be natural or unavoidable responses to stubborn facts (i.e., indissoluble marriage, patriarchal family governance). Locke's family, designed in light of human equality and liberty, encourages critical distance from parental authority but it is grounded in very natural and unavoidable facts that the public has an interest in dealing with as the next generation is produced. Ultimately, Locke's teaching on consent and contract is grounded in the idea that marriage and family life are political institutions—in how they are made and in how they serve the public. He does not take for granted the creation of new citizens in the quest for society's fundamental natural obligation, to perpetuate itself.

Contemporary liberalism denies both of these ideas. It is not the contract and its mode of thinking that led contemporary liberals to embrace privatizing the family, but their denial that nature poses permanent challenges that a culture and a country's institutions should seek to deal with. However, Locke may, in some sense, have contributed to this attitude toward nature. There is an inherent instability in Locke's teaching on the family, derived especially from his treatment of nature. Locke's account of nature's "givens" is prone to shift as we become more able and willing to transform nature's "givens." Institutional connections grounding Locke's sobriety depend on the persistence of several of these "givens"— a man and a woman are necessary for procreation; it is necessary and convenient for fathers and mothers to educate their own children; women need a husband's support during and after pregnancy; and the education provided by families is the most effective way to cultivate self-control and effective citizenship in a liberal polity.

Locke makes arguments for several of these more controversial connections, but he is open in principle to revising them. He does not respect nature, it seems to me, as a created order, but rather as a given or as something that simply is. There may be other ways of connecting these things—though it is not so easy to refute the connections Locke makes. He neither created these particular aspects of nature nor assumed that these aspects of nature could be overcome. It is not Locke's contractual thinking that did marriage in; it is the denial of nature within contemporary liberalism that allowed its contractual ways to become unhinged. It is not liberalism, but the modern attitude toward nature that is the key challenge to family life.

7

LOCKE'S AMBIGUOUS ATTITUDE
TOWARD NATURE

Nasser Behnegar

One of the characteristic features of the modern mind is a certain ambivalence toward nature. This ambivalence is evident in everyday popular attitudes. When we attribute the adjective "natural" to any person or a thing we typically mean it as a sort of praise. And many of us have deep worries about the fate of the natural habitats and of the sustainability of the earth itself, threatened as she seems to be by the unintended consequences of modern technology and economies. On the other hand, we embrace interfering with natural processes (think of birth control pills), the development of artificial products (think of Gore-Tex that clothes so many of us on our camping trips), genetic modification of plants and animals (think of Norman Borlaug's development of a new wheat strain that is credited with saving more than a billion people from starvation), and large-scale modifications of our bodies (sex change or reassignment surgeries). Since these two attitudes are often found in the same minds, they are signs of an ambivalence, and perhaps even of confusion, in regard to our attitude toward nature.

This state of affairs, it seems to me, is the result of a more consistent philosophical attitude toward nature that emerged in the sixteenth and the seventeenth centuries in Europe. For philosophers of antiquity, nature was always a standard by which human institutions or laws were to be judged, a guiding standard even for the arts. The new philosophers, however, conceived of the world in such a way that from the beginning there was a tension between reason and nature. In the more confident expressions of modernity, reason always holds the position of the sovereign whereas the great revolts against modernity, led by Rousseau and Nietzsche, are also, at least in part, attempts to return to nature. But before I discuss the distinctly modern attitude toward nature, I must take you first on a historical tour of the human encounter with nature, beginning with the discovery of nature.

Nature is not to be confused with trees, deer, mountains, rivers, oceans, the earth, etc., that is, with things the thoughts about which are coeval with our experience of them. Nature is rather a special perspective on or insight into such things, an insight that had to be discovered. Accordingly, one may have a rich experience of the world without knowing anything about nature. As Leo Strauss observes, "The Old Testament, whose basic premise may be said to be the implicit rejection of philosophy, does not know 'nature': The Hebrew term for 'nature' is unknown to the Hebrew Bible."[1] According to the same author, the discovery of nature, a discovery that "was made by some Greek twenty-six hundred years ago or before," is coeval with philosophy. Strauss speaks of nature and not merely of the idea of nature, suggesting that the discovery is an insight, albeit an imperfect or incomplete insight, into reality. Moreover, he implies that nature is not merely a presupposition of philosophy but something that once first seen turns the observer into a philosopher because it elicits from the observer the desire for a greater understanding of it. Accordingly, Strauss writes, "the first philosopher was the first man who discovered nature."[2] Now, the first known reference to nature, or in Greek *phusis*, occurs in Homer's *Odyssey* X, 303–6. This is a passage where Odysseus tells the story of his encounter with Hermes who gives him a plant with a power to negate the power of the goddess Circe, who otherwise seemed able to turn Odysseus and his men into pigs. Hermes gives Odysseus the plant and he also shows him its nature: "at its root it was black, but its flower was like milk." This passage suggests that to understand a being like this plant is to understand its nature, which consists of its

---

[1] Leo Strauss, *Natural Right and History* (Chicago: University of Chicago Press, 1953), 81.
[2] Ibid., 82.

essential attributes, its beginning (its root), its end or peak fulfillment (its flower), and implicitly its power (prevention of human
beings being turned into pigs). Now, the power of this plant is sug-
gestive of the essence of nature itself: nature is the essential and unchangeable characteristics of things. The passage also includes a reflection on the connection between the discovery of nature and the
power of gods. According to the wily Odysseus, it is a god who reveals this plant and its nature to him, telling Odysseus that it is difficult for human beings to dig it up but with gods all things are possible. Hermes does not say that it is impossible for human beings to
dig up or discover this plant and the very power of the plant suggests that Hermes, or Odysseus, is not being entirely truthful about
the power of gods. The goddess Circe cannot do anything she pleas-
es when faced with a human being who has ingested this plant or
has knowledge of nature. The discovery of nature then challenges
the omnipotence of gods or, to preserve the ambiguity of the passage, as Strauss does in his gloss on it, nature leads to the reinterpretation of "omnipotence" so that it comes to mean "power limited by
knowledge of 'nature."[3] Now, this thought contradicts the premise
of the Old Testament, which is the free creation of the world by
God through his word or thought. Since everything in the world
owes its whole being, including its power, to God's will, the biblical
view implies that there is nothing in the world that could put a limit
to God's power. God is omnipotent in the full sense of the term.
The basic premise of philosophy contradicts the basic premise of the
Old Testament.

Now, Strauss does not claim that the Bible did not know nature. By referring only to the Old Testament, he suggests that the
New Testament was aware of nature, a suggestion confirmed by the
use of the Greek word for nature in that collection of writings. This
means that Christianity makes uses of two mutually contradictory
premises. It affirms the creation of the world and the omnipotence
implied in it, which omnipotence is central to its promise of resur-
rection of the dead and the hope for everlasting life. But it also finds

---

[3] Ibid., 90.

it necessary to make use of the philosophic premise of nature. This combination is achieved by replacing nature in its original meaning with a nature which itself is the result of creation. "Nature" thus conceived remains a realm of necessity to human beings and the rest of the creation but not to God who can overturn its necessity through his will. This reinterpretation of nature not only does not challenge God's omnipotence but rather becomes a means to distinguish genuine prophecy from false prophecy. If only God can alter nature, the miracles performed by God's prophets become signs that they truly are God's prophets.[4] Similarly, this interpretation of nature may incline pious people toward science, an inclination which was strengthened by the Protestant belief that miracles have ceased with the passing of the age of prophecy. Thus, science becomes one way of getting close to God, for to study nature is to study God's handiwork and his will; it seems that this was the way some of Locke's pious friends, such as Robert Boyle, conceived of their scientific activity.

It seems to me that this combination of creation and nature became necessary to Christianity not so much for theoretical as for moral reasons. It seems that St. Paul's resorting to nature emerged out of his sense of the difficulties that revolve around the promise of Jesus to save human beings from their sins. To sin is to break a law that one knows to be a law. But the Gentiles for the most part had no knowledge of the law that was given to the Hebrews or did not recognize it as a law binding on them. What is more, that law presents itself as a law given to a specific people. Thus, in acting contrary to God's law the Gentiles cannot be viewed as sinners, and not being sinners they would not be in need of redemption or a redeemer. Yet, Paul thinks that the Gentiles appear to recognize the moral parts of the law (in contrast to the judicial or ceremonial parts) as laws binding on them, because when they break these laws they

---

[4] This Christian use of miracles has a precedent in the Old Testament, but the older understanding is complicated on account of its recognition of wonders by forces other than God. Pharaoh's magicians could also perform miracles, but their miracles were less powerful than those of Moses.

sometimes feel remorse. Accordingly, Paul argues that even people who know nothing about the divine scriptures know God's law from their own nature: "For when the Gentiles, which have not the law, do by nature the things contained in the law, these, having not the law, are a law unto themselves: Which show the work of the law written in their hearts, their conscience also bearing witness, and their thoughts the mean while accusing or else excusing one another" (Romans 2:14–15). If it were not for Paul's acceptance of the notion of natural law, a notion articulated first by Greek and Roman philosophers, Christianity would have had to remain a Jewish sect, and not the universal religion that it became. It is also not surprising that natural law became a key concept of Christian thought for more than a thousand years.

The existence of a natural law is evidence for the goodness of nature, for if our nature gives us the law of God, if it is a source of guidance and righteous living, then nature must be a good thing. Christian thought also recognizes even more unambiguously the goodness of the non-human nature. According to the Old Testament, all creation, with the exception of mankind, was judged as good by God (Genesis 1). Once this chapter is read in light of the notion of nature, it becomes evidence for the affirmation of the goodness of the natural world. This nature is not only good in the eyes of God but it is also good for human beings since it is God's gift to mankind. Accordingly, Paul exhorts us to put our trust in "God, who giveth us richly all things to enjoy" (1 Timothy 6: 17; quoted in *Second Treatise*, 31). God's bounty is not only a reason for our gratitude toward him but it also allows us to attend to God's law, specifically the duty to be charitable, without worrying about economic necessity.

Christianity then seems to affirm the goodness of both human and non-human nature. But there is another difficulty in the Christian promise or message that pushes Paul into adopting an entirely contrary attitude toward nature. According to him, in order to be saved one only needs to follow the law: "not the hearers of the law are just before God, but the doers of the law shall be justified" (Romans 2:13). This would seem to mean that those who do obey the law or those who are just do not need to believe in Jesus to be saved. Paul avoids this possibility by contending that "all have sinned, and come short of the glory of God" (Romans 3:23). Now, Paul does not raise so clearly Locke's pointed question, "Why did God give so hard a law to mankind, that to the apostle's time no one of Adam's issues had kept it?"[5] He does, however, suggest an explanation of this state of affairs. If all human beings have failed to keep God's laws, there must be something in human nature that is wicked: "For we know that the law is spiritual: but I am carnal, sold under sin./ For that which I do, I allow not: for what I would, that do I not: but what I hate, that do I" (Romans 7:14–15, King James Version). This attitude is evident in Paul's emphatic hostility toward the flesh and to sexual desire in particular, culminating in his call for celibacy followed by his extraordinary recommendation of marriage for those who cannot be celibate with purity: "it is better to marry than to burn" (1 Corinthians 7:9). In other words, marriage is good not because of so many fine pleasures associated with it but because it weakens sexual desire by assuaging it. In short, Paul and hence the Christian tradition have a complicated and ambivalent attitude toward nature. Our nature teaches us God's law but it prevents us from following that law, at least completely.

Locke's attitude toward nature is informed by elements of both the classical and Christian traditions, but ultimately, it seems to me, he departs in important ways from both traditions. I will begin with a brief sketch of his departure from the classical tradition. To say that nature is good is to imply a fundamental harmony between the natural desires of human beings and the natural world. Now, the goodness of nature is deeply questionable, for there is so much in the natural world that stands in the way of the fulfillment of our natural desires. This difficulty is especially severe for those thinkers such as Plato and Aristotle who recognize the naturalness of the human desire for eternity. How can one reconcile the mortality and limited nature of human beings with their desire for eternity and

---

[5] John Locke, *The Reasonableness of Christianity, as delivered in the Scriptures* (London: C. Baldwin, 1824), 11.

perfection? Nonetheless, by focusing on the satisfaction provided by our highest desire, the desire to know, the classical thinkers accepted the goodness of the world. Elaborating on some comments of Aristotle, Leo Strauss beautifully and succinctly expresses this line of reasoning:

> We cannot exert our understanding without from time to time understanding something of importance; and this act of understanding may be accompanied by the awareness of our understanding, by the understanding of understanding, by *noesis noeseos*, and this is so high, so pure, so noble an experience that Aristotle could ascribe it to his God. This experience is entirely independent of whether what we understand primarily is pleasing or displeasing, fair or ugly. It leads us to realize that all evils are in a sense necessary if there is to be understanding. It enables us to accept all evils which befall us and which may well break our hearts in the spirit of good citizens of the city of God. By becoming aware of the dignity of mind, we realize the true ground of the dignity of man and therewith the goodness of the world, whether we understand it as created or as uncreated, which is the home of man because it is the home of the human mind.[6]

In Locke one also finds a justification of the evils facing human life on account of their necessity for our own good: our vulnerability to pain is a blessing because pain pushes us to take actions that are necessary for our preservation.[7] But, as far as I recall, Locke never justifies evils for the sake of pure understanding. This makes sense given his doubts about the suitability of our mind for understanding the world. According to Locke, all our ideas of the world have their

---

[6] Leo Strauss, *Liberalism Ancient and Modern* (Chicago: University of Chicago Press, 1968), 8.

[7] John Locke, *An Essay Concerning Human Understanding* (Oxford: Oxford University Press, 1975), 129–130. Hereafter referred as *ECHU* followed by book, chapter, and section number. For example, the current passage would be *ECHU* 2.7.4.

origin in our sense perceptions but these perceptions suffer from serious shortcomings. First, our senses capture only some aspects of reality. Accordingly, he speculates about the possibility of the existence of other beings in other parts of the universe that possess senses utterly unknown to us (*ECHU* 2.2.3). Since we lack these potential senses, we are completely closed to those aspects of reality that they disclose, and, of course, what we do not see can deeply affect the meaning of what we do see. Secondly, Locke distinguishes between the primary and the secondary qualities of objects (*ECHU* 2.8). This distinction means that many of our "perceptions," including information very important for our lives such as our perception of tastes, smells, heat, and colors, are not true perceptions, that is, images that resemble the objects of which they are the perception, but merely the effects of those objects on us. Third, all our perceptions are effects of minute particles on our sense organs, minute particles that themselves cannot be perceived by those organs (*ECHU* 2.8.12). These considerations, together with other reflections, seem to have made Locke skeptical of the possibility of a perfect physics or of complete understanding of nature (*ECHU* 4.3.29). Accordingly, Locke emphasizes the practical goals of science rather than its theoretical ones. And to the extent that he still envisages advances in theoretical natural science, which I believe he does, he puts his hopes less on the exercise of our natural faculties than on technological advances such as ever more powerful microscopes. Locke's diminishing of our hopes for theoretical science is accompanied by his fanning of our hopes for the development of a perfect science of ethics, hopes that largely depend on reconceiving morality so that it depends on ideas that are fully conscious constructs of the human mind.[8]

---

[8] Locke's greater confidence in practical reason is also connected with his higher estimation of the value of our senses as guides for action (*ECHU* 2.23.12). We may not understand "fire" but the sensation that it produces when it is in contact with our hands informs us well enough that we should pull our hands away from it. I am grateful to Christopher Bruell for helping me see the importance of the controversy about the status of sense perception in the quarrel between ancient and modern philosophy.

Locke's focus on "practical reason," or on reason as our "Only Star and compass" is very much a consequence of his opposition to superstition and of his engagement with the Christian tradition.[9] This focus is also very much at the heart of his complicated view of nature. For Locke does not simply turn from the supernatural to the natural but to the rational, to a reason that both follows and rules over human nature. One sign of this complication is the bewildering manner in which Locke goes back and forth in characterizing his moral law, sometimes as natural law, other times as law of reason, and on one occasion even simply as reason.

Let us begin with our first or surface impression of Locke, namely, the fact that his political teaching involves a doctrine of natural law. This suggests that his thought is a continuation of the tradition that he inherited. This impression is strengthened by his repeated references to the Bible to confirm his doctrine. But these references have a way of also simultaneously revealing his disagreement with the Christian view. One such relevant passage is his defense of the naturalness of the death penalty as a punishment for murder in the *Second Treatise*, §11: "And *Cain* was so fully convinced, that every one had a Right to destroy such a Criminal, that after the Murther of his Brother, he cries out, *Every one that findeth me, shall slay me*; so plain was it writ in the Hearts of all Mankind." The last phrase of this passage reminds one of that crucial passage from Romans 2:14–15, where Paul informs the reader that God's law is written in the hearts of all men. So it seems that Locke's teaching is perfectly in accord with Paul's. But it turns out that shortly after this comment, Locke maintains that one must be "a studier" of the law of nature in order to know it (*2T* 12). In other words, the law is not written in our hearts but it is something that we need to discover by the use of our reason. Locke makes this point more emphatically in *An Essay Concerning Human Under-*

---

[9] John Locke, *Two Treatises of Government* (Cambridge: Cambridge University Press, 1970) 182-183. Hereafter referred either as *1T* or *2T* followed by the relevant section number. For example, the current passage would be *1T* 58.

standing, where he denies the existence of any innate moral principles. In arguing for this thesis, Locke brings evidence of the general neglect and indifference of whole societies to what his readers would have regarded as basic rules of morality. He argues that even when those rules are accepted by a society they are violated without any sense of remorse in certain situations: "View but an Army at the sacking of a Town, and see what Observation, or Sense of Moral Principles, or what touch of Conscience, for all the Outrages they do. *Robberies, Murders, Rapes*, are the Sports of Men at Liberty from Punishment and Censure" (*ECHU* I.3.9). Locke's denial of innate moral principles is simply incompatible with Paul's doctrine announced in his letters to the Romans.

But if the law is not written in our hearts by nature, we must conclude that for Locke nature is less good to man than the Christian tradition suggested, and since nature is viewed as the creation of God, the demotion of the goodness of nature has an anti-theological implication. Locke draws our attention to this when he considers a possible objection to his denial of innate moral principles, including an innate notion of God: "it is urged, That it is *Suitable to the goodness of God, to imprint, upon the Minds of Men, characters and Notions of himself,* and not to leave them in the dark, and doubt, in so grand a Concernment; and also by that means, to secure to himself the Homage and Veneration, due from so intelligent a Creature as Man; and therefore he has done it" (*ECHU* 1.4.12). In response, Locke argues that it is a bad argument to suppose that because we think it would be good for God to have done something it proves that he has done it. While Locke does not deny the premise that whatever God does must be good, he does not even attempt to show how God's decision not to imprint an image of himself in the souls of men is good. He simply argues that there is no evidence that God has done this. He thus leaves those of his readers who accept his thesis that there are no innate moral principles with the choice of supposing that God's decision must have served some mysterious good unfathomable to human beings or to wonder about the goodness of God, and hence about the existence of God as he was understood by the Christian tradition.

The question of the goodness of God is inseparable from one's judgment about divine providence. At the outset of the *Two Treatises* Locke recognizes the order found in the world as a reflection of God's will by noting a threefold ambiguity in Filmer's reference to God's appointment, for "whatsoever providence orders, or the law of nature directs, or positive Revelation declares, may be said to be *by God's Appointment*" (*1T* 16). Now, if obedience to God's will is the core of morality, the acceptance of the political arrangement into which one is born would be a moral duty. Accordingly, a number of Christian thinkers have argued that one should obey one's sovereign even if he is a tyrant because he was placed in his position by God, whether it be to punish us or for some other reason unknown to us. Of course, the main political thesis of the *Two Treatises*—the right to fight against tyrants—contradicts this line of reasoning. That Locke rejects not only the conclusion of this argument but also its basic premise is evident from an important moment in his discussion of the meaning of God's curse on Eve at Genesis 3:16. After raising a number of objections against the view that this verse makes Adam sovereign over Eve and thus over all human beings generated by them, Locke denies that this curse was a punishment, and he does so by denying it would be morally wrong for Eve and other women to escape it: "there is no more Law to oblige a Woman to such a Subjection, if the Circumstances either of her Condition or Contract with her Husband should exempt her from it, [than] there is, that she should bring forth her Children in Sorrow and Pain, if there could be found a Remedy for it, which is also a part of the same Curse upon her" (*1T* 47). This verse is not a punishment but an expression of God's providence that has its foundation in the natural differences between men and Women: "God, in this Text, gives not, that I see, any Authority to *Adam* over *Eve*, or to Men over their Wives, but only foretels what should be the Womans Lot, how by his Providence he would order it so, that she should be subject to her husband, as we see that generally the Laws of Mankind and custom of Nations have ordered it so; and there is, I grant, a Foundation in Nature for it" (*1T* 47). These two statements together imply that it is morally permissible and even wise to overthrow

God's providence if one is in a position to do so. And since providence has its foundation in nature, the latter can no longer simply fulfill the place that it has for classical thinkers. Our nature, at least the nature of women, is in some aspects a kind of curse. It is telling that for Locke as for Nietzsche the modern understanding of the problem of nature reveals itself most clearly in the case of the nature of women. For Locke, women are by nature unlucky in the sense that they are born "the weaker sex," but they are free to undo as much as they can their natural curse. Nietzsche, on the other hand, in the last phase of his thought affirms the inequality of the sexes in a language more stridently harsh than anything found in premodern philosophers precisely because he wants to restore nature as the standard but only on the modern grounds or without affirming the goodness of nature.

To return to Locke, there is a tension between §47 of the *First Treatise*, where he says that no law obliges a woman to be subject to her husband "if the Circumstances either of her Condition or Contract with her Husband should exempt her from it," and §82 of the *Second Treatise* where after he acknowledges the inevitability of disagreements between husband and wife and the necessity of someone in the family deciding the issues, he argues that the rule "naturally falls to the Man's share, as the abler and stronger." How are we to understand this contradiction? It seems to me wrong to deny that the latter treatment is empty of normative consequences. I do think he means to suggest that by nature men should generally rule in a marriage. Any association that is to last, he argues, must have a way of resolving disagreements, and since marriage is an association of two, the method of majority rule, a method that works for civil society, cannot be applied to it. There are only two options: to place the rule in the female or the male partner. But since the female partner is less able to take care of herself for significant periods of time on account of pregnancy, and since she is unable to overpower her mate, to give the rule to her is to create an association that is doomed to fail. Locke's preference for male rule in marriage is an inference from the nature of the association. But as Locke's discussion of marriage in the *First Treatise* shows, there can be circumstances that overturn this natural order, circumstances that would make it reasonable for the female partner to have the rule. It is likely that Locke has in mind particular circumstances that qualify the general rule, but a question arises whether it would be reasonable to alter the circumstances of women as a class with the view of increasing their power in marriage. As far as I know, Locke does not address this question, the answer to which would surely depend on his assessment of the true interests of both women and men. But it seems to me that Locke would not necessarily object to such efforts in principle, that is, without reflecting on the consequences of such efforts, for he conceives of nature as a set of conditional necessities which are only ambiguously connected with human happiness. For Locke nature does serve as some sort of standard but it is not the ultimate standard. The ultimate standard is reason and the quest for human happiness.

Locke's openness to the alteration of nature manifests itself most clearly in his doctrine of the state of nature. He makes two opposing suggestions about this. On one hand, it seems to be a state in which men live according to reason, and thus "a State of peace, Good will, Mutual Assistance, and Preservation" (2T 19). On the other hand, the great reason that man must leave the state of nature is to avoid the state of war, which suggests at the very least that the state of nature inevitably leads to the state of war. Let us see how it happens. According to Locke, men living in the state of nature are under the law of nature which Locke equates with reason, and since law is utterly useless without someone executing it and thus punishing those who break the law, and since in the state of nature everyone is equal, it follows that in the state of nature everyone has the right to punish others for violating the dictates of reason. Now, Locke acknowledges an objection to his position: "To this strange Doctrine, viz. That in *the State of Nature, every one has the Executive Power* of the Law of Nature, I doubt not but it will be objected, That it is unreasonable for Men to be Judges in their own Cases, that Self-Love will make Men partial to themselves and their Friends. And on the other side, that Ill Nature, Passion and Revenge will carry them too far in punishing others. And Hence nothing but Confusion and Disorder will follow, and that therefore God hath certainly appointed Government to restrain the partiality and violence of Men" (*2T* 13). Locke's response to this objection makes it clear that, apart from the conclusion that God has appointed Government, he agrees with everything else. The natural condition of man is self-contradictory, for nature recognizes reason as the only legislative power and yet it puts human beings in an unreasonable situation, where reason is either not developed or lacks the power to rule human beings. To remove this contradiction, to put man in a more rational situation, one must enter a civil government, which in Locke's reading cannot be done without agreement or convention, and without leaving the state of nature.

I have argued that Paul's ambivalence toward nature consists of his recognition of natural conscience as a source of moral law and his denunciation of our natural appetites. Locke's ambivalence is almost the inverse of Paul's. Nature is a more ambiguous source of guidance for him than it is for Paul or the classical thinkers. The state of nature is not a model for civil society; it guides its construction the way a problem calls for a solution. Whereas for Paul the non-human natural world is a rich gift of God, for Locke "Nature and the Earth furnish only the almost worthless Materials, as in themselves" (*2T* 43). Much of nature's value depends on its potentiality to serve as material for human labor. Nonetheless, it would be wrong to say that Locke completely abandons nature as a positive source of guidance. There are some natural inclinations that are either not wise or impossible to suppress: "Nature, I confess, has put into Man a desire for Happiness, an aversion to Misery: These indeed are innate practical Principles, which (as practical Principles ought) do continue constantly to operate and influence all our Actions, without ceasing" (*ECHU* 1.3.3). There are natural desires that are inseparable from our good and Locke suggests that reason must give priority to these desires over other natural desires that may serve ends other than one's good. Thus, in Locke nature does not completely lose its status as a standard.

Although no one has ever accused Locke's philosophy for encouraging sexual desires, Locke is much more tolerant of the lower or the common human appetites than Paul. For instance, while making the argument for the rule of the majority in the formation of government, Locke argues that to demand universal consent "would be only like *Cato's* coming into Theatre, only to go out again" (*2T* 98). Cato's pure taste, a taste that does not tolerate lewdness, is incompatible with political life in the sense of being a rule for politics. Locke not only tolerates some of the lower human appetites, he encourages others, including the desire to accumulate money as much as possible, within legal restriction, because such pursuits are productive of the general good of mankind. Yet it is misleading to say that Locke completely unleashes human passions. According to him, human labor is by far the greatest source of the value of things that are necessary or useful or convenient to human life. Since labor is the source of value and power, Locke praises as wise and godlike the Prince who "by establishing laws of liberty secures protection and incouragment to the honest industry of Mankind" (*2T* 42). The industrious person becomes the new ideal of humanity: "God has given the World to Men in Common, but since he gave it for their benefit, and the greatest Conveniences of Life they were capable to draw from, it cannot be supposed he meant that it should always remain common and uncultivated. He gave it to the use of the Industrious and Rational (and Labour was to be his Title to it) not to the Fancy or Covetousness of the Quarrelsome and Contentious" (*2T* 34). Now, industriousness is not limited to commercial activity, for in describing his own philosophic work, Locke frequently refers to his pain, his labor, and he even describes himself as a kind of day-laborer removing rubbish out of the way of the progress of science. Industry involves labor and labor is a kind of pain, but pain is something that by nature human beings seek to avoid. The new Ideal then requires human beings to go against the grain of their own nature, at least to a considerable extent. In conclusion, Locke's ideal involves a kind of asceticism, but a peculiar one, for its overcoming of nature presupposes a continuous and never to be forgotten contact with nature (think of his very doctrine of the state of nature) and because of this some aspects of nature and the value of nature are preserved in Locke's thought. This confirms the observation of

Max Weber, who noted the ascetic character of modernity, but we add that Locke's asceticism is not a mere secularization of Christianity. His asceticism is fundamentally different from Christian asceticism because it is not a form of self-denial and because the idea of natural necessity is preserved in it. The desire to preserve oneself, which plays so fundamental a role in Locke's political philosophy, is, according to him, the strongest natural desire, even if its mere naturalness may no longer be the basis of Locke's respect for it.

INDEX

Singer, Natasha 158n
Smith, Adam 138, 148-9
Smith, Samuel Harrison 137
Sreenivasan, Gopal 17n
Stone, Lawrence 162n
Strauss, Leo 89, 104n, 116n,
    130n, 132n, 176-7, 181
Swann, Marjorie 97n, 99n,
    101n
Sypherd, W.O. 97n, 98n, 100n
Takayama, Noriyuki 161n
Tarcov, Nathan 20n, 35n, 131n
Thompson, John L. 85n, 96n,
    97n, 98n
Tocqueville, Alexis de 7, 150
Tyack, David B. 137n
Uriah 101
Vanderheiden, Steve 164n
Vaughn, Benjamin 151
Waldmann, Felix 45n, 46n,
    55n, 56n
Walmsley, J.C. 45n, 46n, 55n,
    56n
Ward, Lee 14n, 15n, 25n, 38n,
    39n, 69n, 73n
Warnick, Melody 157n
Washington, George 160
Weber, Max 190
Webster, Noah 151
Werding, Martin 161n
Westover, Tara 135n
Wolff, Robert Paul 2n
Wolfson, Adam 43n, 60n
Wolseley, Charles 45-6, 48-51,
    57
Yaffe, Gideon 10n
Yenor, Scott 5, 159, 163n, 166n
Zimmerman, Carle C. 162n
Zuckert, Michael P. 1n, 10n,
    15n, 17n, 33n, 36n

Zvesper, John 33n